GOODHART

1st Edition

Published in 2012 by
Woodfield Publishing Ltd
Bognor Regis PO21 5EL England
www.woodfieldpublishing.co.uk

ISBN 1-84683-146-6

Printed and bound in England

Typesetting & page design: Nik Pastorius
Cover design: Klaus Berger

Goodhart

The story of an exceptional man

RICHARD HARRIS &
BARRIE WILLIAMS

Woodfield

Woodfield Publishing Ltd

Bognor Regis ~ West Sussex ~ England ~ PO21 5EL
tel 01243 821234 ~ **e/m** info@woodfieldpublishing.co.uk

Interesting and informative books on a variety of subjects

For full details of all our published titles, visit our website at
www.woodfieldpublishing.co.uk

I would like to dedicate this book to my beloved wife Molly who has, these past few years, encouraged me to 'get on with it.' Without her, I would not have got on with it!
Nicholas Goodhart
(Written shortly before his death in April, 2011)

~ CONTENTS ~

Foreword ~ *by David Ince*

THROUGHOUT HIS LONG LIFE and many interests, Nicholas Goodhart was above all the complete aviator; ranked amongst those in our armed forces who are destined for the highest command. A member of that rare and valued breed an engineering test pilot, he was also a world-class gliding champion and no mean inventor in his later years. Nicholas Goodhart was a truly remarkable man

In the 1930s whilst training at Dartmouth, and then at Keyham, the Naval Engineering College, we catch a first glimpse of his growing attachment to 'soaring flight' and his encounters with the great Robert Kronfeld. Later, when he and I were together at the Empire Test Pilots School (ETPS), Kronfeld came to tell us about the Airborne Forces Experimental Establishment. Nicholas wanted to get him to talk about gliding and was much frustrated that his brief had been limited to dreary projects like aerotowed guns and winged jeeps!

How he moved from air engineering to test pilot is a story in itself. After an active and singularly dangerous two years in the Med – and an incredible Fred Karno performance convoying 28 Landing Craft Tanks (LCTs) back to the UK for the invasion of Normandy – he reported to the Admiralty and found himself posted for flying training. This led to a tour on Hellcats over Burma with a ditching, following engine failure, over the Malacca Straits.

How he subsequently made it to the first ETPS post war course with just 400 plus flying hours remains shrouded in mystery. Those who know him well might guess that he used his engineering background and debating skills to beat the many naval aviators with far more flying time and experience. At ETPS he soon proved that their Lordships had made a wise decision.

After watching helplessly from above, as Pete Garner was killed in the prototype Wyvern, the way in which Nicholas volunteered to take over the testing is typical of this splendid man as we come to know him better. His feelings of loss, his courage, and his sense of responsibility are reflected forever in that decision to pick up the torch from his friend.

As we move on to gliding his actions, his achievements and the stories of his record breaking flights speak for themselves. Gliding brought further challenges, on the ground and in the air. As a member of the BGA Council and chairman of the Airspace Committee he fought many battles to protect us from the ever encroaching demands of the National Air Traffic Control Service and the airlines. Perhaps his greatest single achievement as Airspace Boss, an apt description, was that of helping to win the Lasham Gliding Society's vitally needed long term security of tenure.

In the early summer of 1971, with a magnificent championship winning record of over 20 years to his name, Nicholas won the British Standard Class Championships. By now he was becoming less enamoured with high performance soaring unless it was in direct competition with others. In August that year, on a superb gliding day, I caught him listening out on the radio from his home at Inkpen. 'Old warhorses,' he said, 'stir at the sound of the trumpets!'

The following year, at the World Championships in Yugoslavia, he was 4th in the Open Class, just off the podium. It was a fitting conclusion to a great gliding career.

Richard Harris and Barrie Williams have done a splendid job in tracking the highlights of his life. Not least his great inventive achievements which are covered in accurate and comprehensive detail – the Mirror Deck Landing System, Sigma with its variable geometry wings, the Newbury Manflyer, Albedo, the giant 3km span Hurricane suppressor and its forest firefighting derivative on which Nicholas was still working at the time of his death.

The authors were still working with Nicholas on this book when he died and consequently it is unfortunate that we miss out on some events from the later years of his Naval career.

Yet largely thanks to his treasured and dearest Molly, his wife and best friend – we encounter something much more revealing. A wonderful partnership, a most loving marriage, a family man at peace with himself and the world. The driving force is still there – in a totally different way – as we see more clearly than ever the warmth, the humour, the kindness and the caring of her Nicholas.

It is there in his year as Master of the Worshipful Company of Grocers, the sixth Goodhart to be so honoured – as a powerfully effective and innovative name at Lloyds – in his contribution to the Lindridge Estate development, a sort-of top rank surveyor to the Irish builder – who trusted him implicitly – waterworks and all! We see it in the man who, on his first visit to the Children's Hospice South West, played with the little ones and wept silently for them. Who devoted much of his last years to that charity – who at 88 became a spritely youngster himself – abseiling down a 120ft church tower and raising £4,200 for its funds.

Nicholas – dear friend and comrade – what a privilege it is to have known you. What a man and what a life!

As the Last Post is most surely followed by Reveille, and the final bugle call fades into silence, I shall remember you – always.

David Ince flew almost 150 sorties – earning a DFC on the way – after being seconded from the Royal Artillery to become a World War II fighter pilot. After the war he trained as a test pilot at the Empire Test Pilots School, where he met Nicholas Goodhart, who became a lifelong friend.

Preface ~ *by Simon Hoggart*

I DIDN'T GET OFF TO the very best start with Nicholas Goodhart when we first met 30 years ago. His wife Molly told me, with justifiable pride, that he was about to become Master of the Grocers Company.

Lacking any knowledge of London's grand livery companies – and few are grander than the Grocers – I assumed he was a sort of top grocer, like Lord Sainsbury for example. I said I didn't know that he was in the retail trade. I was very soon put right and since then I have been able to enjoy the magnificent hospitality at Grocers' Hall and admire their tremendous good works.

What a man of achievement Nicholas was!

A trainee cadet at the age of 13, he joined the Royal Navy, served during the war and worked as an engineer on weapons systems. Before then he had taken up his great love, gliding – he flew in nine British championships, winning three firsts and three seconds – and his two seater sailplane record still stands, though admittedly the class has now been abolished.

Once, when Nicholas and Molly were travelling in France, their camper van was robbed and, without money or credit cards, they had set off trying to get home. They noticed a British car behind them, towing a glider. They flagged the vehicle down and discovered that it was being driven by a huge fan of Nicholas who was only too happy to lend them the money they needed.

Nicholas's record of achievement is astonishing. He was a fighter pilot during the Burma campaign, a test pilot at Boscombe Down and a continuous innovator in aircraft design.

His greatest and best-known achievement came in the mid 1950s with the mirror-deck landing system. At the time, propeller driven planes were being replaced by larger, heavier, faster jets. Landing these on an aircraft carrier with an angled deck was far more difficult, especially as pilots had to be guided by a man waving what appeared to be two table-tennis bats. It was human error turned into military strategy.

Like all Nicholas's best ideas, it was very simple. The pilot had to adjust his angle of descent so that the light appeared to be in the centre of the mirror.

In that way he could hold the glide slope, more precisely, all the way to touchdown. It reduced the rate of attrition hugely and saved hundreds of lives – not to mention hundreds of planes. No wonder it was quickly adopted by every nation that had aircraft carriers and no wonder the United States awarded him the Legion of Merit shortly afterwards.

There were other inventions, too. Many were of the '*Why on earth didn't I think of that?*' variety such as the box junction. He sent the idea to the old Ministry of Transport; lo and behold, a few years later they appeared on our roads but he received neither payment nor acknowledgment. I remember once trying to work out with him how much he would have earned if he had only one-hundredth of one penny for each car that crossed a box junction. He would have made Bill Gates look like a church mouse by comparison.

In the 1970s he invented the Newbury Manflyer, a human-powered aircraft made largely of balsa wood and powered by two men frantically pedalling bicycles. In those days, when the computing power we now have in a small laptop had to be housed in vast rooms like aircraft hangars, he 'borrowed' the huge computer at Farnborough and worked through the night on his calculations. The plane worked well; it flew, though not very far and finally it crashed. The Americans won the prize for crossing the channel but the BBC made a moving film about the Manflyer and if you ever get to watch it you'll see family and friends eagerly crawling under and over the plane as they helped to build it.

Nicholas was always working on something. I remember him visiting us while we lived in Washington and he was employed by Boeing. He played with our baby daughter while working on a device that would squeeze the air out of two-litre plastic bottles, keeping tonic water fizzy and saving, oh I don't know, pennies a day. He gave up when the thing had reached a size only slightly smaller than a wardrobe. His mechanised corkscrew didn't work either – or rather, it would have done if it hadn't weighed roughly twice as much as the bottle of wine it was supposed to open!

He never stopped inventing. Even in the year before he died he was working on a plane with a wingspan of three kilometres. It was to be a hurricane-buster, dropping a lid on embryo hurricanes as they formed in the ocean. An acquaintance of his in the Met Office told him that it wouldn't work so, quite undaunted, he started to convert it into a forest fire buster.

Those of us privileged to know Nicholas remember him not just as an inventor but as a warm, charming man who loved his life: his long walks, good conversation – often combative – a glass of wine with his dinner and port or Madeira afterwards; his lovely home and most of all Molly, his beloved wife of nearly 40 years, who provided such a wonderful setting for his life and his work. Their house was also a second home for so many of his now extended family, especially his step-children and their seven children. He was a marvellous step-father and step-grandfather and in these days of extended families, I cannot think of a finer role model.

Nicholas never read a novel in his life – *'waste of time,'* he would say, *'none of it actually happened.'* But he was fascinated by the factual.

Tact was not, perhaps, his middle name. In America, he was shown around the house of our next door neighbour who was very proud of his modern art collection. *'I'm afraid I don't like these,'* Nicholas told him. *'They don't look like anything. I prefer photographs.'* But he said it with that engaging, cheeky grin which made everyone forgive him everything.

It was a privilege to know such a man; a privilege no-one who knew him will ever forget. And if I close my eyes I can still see that warm and mischievous grin.

Simon Hoggart, renowned journalist, Guardian *columnist, TV and radio broadcaster, is the husband of Nicholas Goodhart's stepdaughter, Alyson.*

About the Authors

BARRIE WILLIAMS' 40-year journalistic career includes the Editorship of three major regional newspapers – the *Kent Evening Post,* the *Nottingham Evening Post* and the *Western Morning News.* His acclaimed biography of legendary soccer star Tommy Lawton **Get In There!** *(Vision Sports Publishing)* was shortlisted in the British Sports Book Awards for 2011 and nominated for William Hill Sports Book of The Year.

His autobiography **Ink In The Blood** was published by *Woodfield in 2007* and he also wrote **Somebody Had To Do It** *(Authorhouse)* – a biography of notorious print industry 'Union Buster' Christopher Pole-Carew.

RICHARD HARRIS spent 25 years on provincial newspapers, rising to become Assistant Editor of the *Nottingham Evening Post* and then Editor of the *Evening News & Star* and weekly *Cumberland News* in Carlisle before becoming a freelance journalist in Cumbria.

His autobiography **The Accidental Editor** – so named because he grew up wanting to go to sea and never intended to be a journalist in the first place – is published by Authorhouse and is available at www.theaccidentaleditor.com

Acknowledgements

WE ARE GRATEFUL for the invaluable help and encourage-
ment provided by many people in the writing of this book –
not least Nicholas Goodhart's widow Molly and the rest of his
extended family. Also our thanks go to Lance Cole (author of
Secrets of the Spitfire) for his assistance with the chapter on the
Sigma glider; to Simon Grant and Tony Wing for their memo-
ries of their days as pilots of the Newbury Manflyer; to the
British Gliding Association, for confirming details of Nicholas
Goodhart's gliding career; to *Sailplane & Gliding* and the
Admiralty for providing photographs; to the RN Disclosure
Cell at Portsmouth for their help in accessing Nicholas's Royal
Navy files; and most of all to Nicholas's old friend David Ince
for his patient and painstaking efforts in ensuring that we got
things right.
  Barrie Williams & Richard Harris

1.   Goodhart the record breaker

HIS FEET WERE SO COLD he hardly knew they were there. Cold and numb, hidden deep down in the nose of his small aircraft, where the warmth from the blazing sun that beat down through the canopy on to his upper body could never reach. Strange, he thought, how they could be so very cold while the rest of his body was so very hot. He must somehow stop them getting too cold, because then he would not be able to move them and without feet he would not be able operate the rudder properly. And if he couldn't do that... well, then he could be in trouble. Seven miles above the ground is no place to lose control of your feet when you're in an aeroplane without an engine.

He eased the stick to the left, a movement he matched with a little pressure from his icy left foot on the pedal. The glider swung gently towards the west, towards the mountains... and towards the feat that would write his name in the history books of aviation for ever.

It was early May 1955 and Nicholas Goodhart had achieved much in his 36 years. A Commander in the Royal Navy, a test pilot, a highly qualified engineer, the inventor of a device which even then had saved the lives of countless airmen... in aviation circles he was already something of a household name. But this was something different, something that many of his fellow glider pilots looked upon as the ultimate challenge...

He intended to fly higher than any British glider pilot had ever flown before.

His friend Bill Ivans, an American champion glider pilot, had arranged an expedition to Bishop, California – to the mountains of Sierra Nevada and its powerful standing waves. In recent years these had helped gliders to reach extraordinary altitudes. Bill had done as much preparation as possible – equipping his Schweizer SGS 1-23 with a high capacity oxygen system and arranging for another friend to bring his Cessna to tow the glider into the air.

They woke on the morning of May 9th to find the wind blowing strongly from the west, bringing with it the wave so beloved of top-class glider pilots. Nicholas and Bill knew it was the opportunity for which they had been waiting. It was their first – and very possibly their last – chance.

Bill went first (it was his glider, after all!) but, despite the flying prowess that had made him one of America's top glider pilots, was back all too soon. He reported a barely credible turbulence on tow towards the mountains, both aircraft being buffeted by violent up and down drafts as they headed in the direction of the 14,000ft peaks of Mount Humphreys. Despite the skills he had acquired from years of flying in that part of California he had failed to connect with the wave and, begrudgingly admitting defeat, had to return to the airfield a disappointed man.

At least, this left the way clear for Nicholas... He delayed his launch long enough for a detailed de-briefing by his friend so he knew all about the turbulence, the strange absence of any rising air where he would expect it and the frustration of returning to earth with the job not done.

But as the tow plane powered forward along the runway, with the glider following obediently in its wake, Nicholas knew his chances of achieving the success that had eluded his friend were slim. Equally, he knew that he would probably never get a better chance. It was, if not now or never, now or not for a very long time and that was something he did not care to contemplate.

As the two aircraft gained height, one behind the other, he found that the conditions were even worse than he expected. Bill had warned him about the turbulence and turbulence was something he was always prepared for – disturbed air like that has to be overcome on the climb up towards even a modest wave. But this time it was different.

He struggled to keep the glider under control as it followed the Cessna through the sky. The turbulence would roll the tow plane 90 degrees to the right, with the glider following suit a second or two later despite Nicholas's attempts to keep it level by easing the stick to the left. Then the turbulence would roll the tow plane 90 degrees to the left, leaving him struggling to stay in position, both vertically and horizontally. Were he to get too high or too low he could over-ride the Cessna pilot's control. Too high and he would drag the Cessna nose down. Too low and he risked stalling the glider, with roughly the same potentially disastrous result.

The glider was being tossed around in the sky like a twig in the waters of a rock-strewn river. The turbulence was more severe than anything he had ever known, more severe than anything he had ever imagined, and it was threatening to bring his adventure to an early end.

Then suddenly it was over. Pure bliss! It was as if he had broken through a plate glass window and landed on a piece of thick velvet on the other side. The turbulence had gone and the air was so smooth there was not a sound as the glider cut effortlessly across the sky. He pulled the cable release . . . the tug dived away . . . and he was on his own.

He turned the glider into the wind, looked down and chose a pinnacle among the mountains immediately beneath him and then adjusted his air speed so that he maintained his position over it. To anyone on the ground looking up he would have appeared to be hovering like a giant bird of prey.

If it had not been for the variometer – a very sensitive vertical speed indicator which showed him how quickly the glider was rising – he would hardly have been conscious of any movement at all.

But moving he was – upwards and fast. Quickly, he clasped the mask over his face and turned on the essential oxygen. He knew that for pilots flying at above 10,000ft pure oxygen was advisable and that at above 15,000ft it was essential. He was well above that now. The altimeter was winding furiously – 20,000ft, 25,000ft, 30,000ft – and although the variometer showed that the climb had slowed somewhat from the extraordinary 10 knots (1,000ft per minute) it had displayed a few minutes earlier, he was still gaining height.

Then suddenly it was there – the magic figure! 37,000ft. Spell it out: Thirty seven thousand feet. Well past the greatest height that that any British pilot had previously achieved in a glider. Other men might have let out a whoop of delight, clenched their fists or rejoiced with a quick verse of *God Save The Queen*, but not Nicholas Goodhart. That wasn't his style. To mark such a momentous achievement, an achievement for which he had worked so hard and so long, there was virtually nothing. 'Smug satisfaction is about as far as I go,' he said later.

The record was his so quickly on that flight, and in the end so easily attained, he now had the rest of the afternoon to fill. Which meant he had plenty of time to enjoy the view. Unlike the airliners busy about their business below him, in which passengers have to sit with their noses pressed against the glass to catch a fleeting view of the land below, a glider's cockpit gives a pilot almost all-round vision and Nicholas was making the most of it. The snow-covered Sierra Nevada was spread out beneath him, glistening in the brilliant sunshine on its highest peaks. To the south-west the Pacific Ocean ran deep blue all the way to the horizon; to the west the tall buildings of San Francisco led the eye to the iconic Golden Gate bridge and to the south was the urban sprawl of Los Angeles, a grim blot on the landscape even from that height. Of human activity there was little to be seen. A little traffic here and a train or two there, and the occasional commercial airliner somewhere far below – but it was an astonishingly peaceful scene, far removed from the bustle of normal American life.

Nicholas was entranced. It was something only glider pilots can enjoy and precious few even of them had been privileged to witness anything quite like this. But he was also cold, or at least his feet were. Even though it was getting late in the day now, there was still plenty of warmth from the sun on his head and on his shoulders but with the high altitude bringing the temperature outside the glider to around minus 40 his feet – which, being tucked into the aluminium nose of the aircraft, had been in the shade all along – were beginning to freeze.

He had known it was going to be cold – high altitudes in an aircraft with no heating were always cold, even with the sun blazing fiercely into the cockpit – so he had wrapped himself up well for the occasion. A couple of pairs of long johns, thick stockings and a pair of electric socks, flying boots, blue jeans, vest, open-neck shirt, a woolly scarf, a sunhat and thick gloves... But none of that was much protection against the bitter cold that was starting to gnaw away at his toes.

He wondered how he would manage to get home safely, because glider pilots need both feet to operate the rudder. Sooner or later he would have to land and landing without full control of the glider... well, that could be a problem. It is only the delicate use of the rudder that stops the aircraft skidding dangerously across the sky when it turns left or right, which is not so important when you're flying at 37,000ft but is potentially catastrophic when you're making your final turn and heading for the landing strip at 60mph.

Then the calm scientific logic for which Nicholas Goodhart was well known began to take over. It's not feet you need to operate the rudder pedals, he rationalised. It's not even legs. Your legs and feet simply act as pushrods to transmit the force to the rudder pedal, so as long as your thigh muscles are in working order it doesn't much matter how frozen your feet and lower legs are.

Problem solved! So he thought no more about it and continued what was turning into one of the best flights of his life.

It was only when he saw the street lights being turned on in Bishop, the town seven miles below, that he began to think vaguely of heading back to the landing site, back to Bill. Street lights? Dusk? Approaching night? He'd been so enchanted by the view he had lost all track of time. He turned the glider to where he thought the down side of the wave would be so he could use the falling air to help speed his descent. But it wasn't there. He tried again and still couldn't find it. The wave was still sending him upwards, away from the ground where very soon he would need to be.

He grasped the air brake lever and pulled hard. The glider began to lose height, but it was exceptionally hard work, even for a fit man like Nicholas. The air brakes were spring-loaded so he had to keep pulling on the lever, first with one hand then, when that one got tired, with the other; if he let go the brakes would snap shut and cease to operate and the glider would start climbing again.

At this rate, he thought, it will take a full hour to reach the ground. By then it will be pitch dark and landing at an airfield which had no lights was not an attractive proposition. Even landing in the half-dark was not something he would ever choose to do but he knew that on this occasion he had no alternative.

As Nicholas slowly lost height circling the airfield, by now hidden in the gloom, he realised he had reckoned without the ingenuity of his friends. He noticed scurrying activity on the ground, people bustling around the cars parked near the landing strip. Then he understood what they were doing – they were going to use the lights of their cars to guide him home.

Two cars were parked just short of the point at which he needed to touch down, with their headlights pointing along the runway upon which he was to land. He had to fly over the cars, land just past them and come to a halt a short distance beyond.

For a pilot of Nicholas's experience accomplishing a decent landing in such circumstances, unusual though they were, was fairly straightforward and he achieved it almost perfectly.

As the glider rolled to a halt in the near dark he allowed himself another moment of 'smug satisfaction'. He had been right. Glider pilots do indeed need only their thigh muscles to operate the rudder, so it doesn't matter if they can't feel their feet. But having brought the glider back safely to terra firma presented new problems.

He was so cold he could not get out.

His friends who ran over and gathered around to congratulate him on such an extraordinary flight found he could barely move. They had to help him to remove the canopy then lift him from the cockpit and carry him bodily to the flying club's clubhouse. It was only there, with a mug of steaming hot coffee in his hands and an electric fire at his feet that he began slowly to thaw out. His feet – the soles of which were frozen quite literally to blocks of ice – had to be thawed over the electric fire and that was no fun at all. The pain in his feet was intense and they never fully recovered. Even in old age he still had cold feet, even in a room heated to more than 70 degrees Fahrenheit.

But who cares about cold feet when he knows he has just flown into the record books? Not Nicholas Goodhart. He had the trace from his barograph, the instrument which records precisely how high an aircraft has been. The official calibration showed 37,050ft. This was higher than any other British glider pilot had ever flown. He had done it.

And it was a record that was to stand for more than 40 years.

2.   Goodhart the boy

THERE WAS NOTHING about the boy Nicholas Goodhart to suggest that one day he might be setting world records in an exacting and sometimes death-defying sport like gliding. He was a rather sickly child who hated physical activity and dreaded school sports. He felt permanently poorly, suffering from frequent headaches, and whenever he tried to play football or hockey it made him feel even worse. Many years later this was to be diagnosed as migraine but in the 1920s he was simply labelled 'bilious'.

Hilary Charles Nicholas Goodhart had made a typically orderly entry into the world on 28th September 1919. The third son of Mr and Mrs Gavin Caird Goodhart, he was born on the 120-acre family estate at Inkpen in Berkshire.

There is only one true family of Goodharts in the United Kingdom, stemming from Jakob Emanuel Guthardt, who came to England in the Court of King George II in 1755 and anglicised his name. In the early 1900s an anglophile American professor changed his name to Goodhart and started a new strain, but Nicholas's father came from the main stream of the family who made their money in sugar importing and insurance. They are the principal family in the Worshipful Company of Grocers, the number two City of London Livery Company.

The Company was established in 1345 as the Guild of Pepperers, which had first been known in 1180 and was responsible for maintaining standards for the purity of spices. In 1515 the

Court of Aldermen of the City of London decreed an order of precedence for the 48 livery companies then in existence, based on each company's economic or political power.

The Worshipful Company of Grocers is, to this day, out-ranked only by The Worshipful Company of Mercers.

One story (probably apocryphal) has it that the Grocers' Company used to be first in the order until the day Queen Victoria, offended because the Grocers' ceremonial camel had emitted unfortunate odours during a procession, promoted the Mercers.

Gavin Caird Goodhart, born in 1882, was reserved by nature. He was a natural and extremely skilled engineer, which made him a misfit because, in the 19th Century, numeracy was social-ly unacceptable to respectable people and a decent education meant the classics.

Gavin grew up in the family mansion called Langley Park in what is now South London but was, at the time, open country and his father resolved that he should be educated at Harrow, from where he was expected to go to university. There was no little disappointment when, instead, he chose to become an apprentice at one of the new electricity companies which were springing up to supply the capital. There, he learned electrical engineering.

When the First World War intervened, Gavin served as an armourer in the Royal Naval Air Service but never went to sea, spending his war on the Western Front instead.

Back home from the war, he found that his role as a country gentleman did not satisfy him, so he converted a large barn into a workshop, which he equipped with all he needed to make anything he chose. Power came from an old one-cylinder petrol engine with unguarded, flapping belts.

That workshop was a place of wonder to Gavin's children, Tony, Kit, Nicholas and the youngest, daughter Anstace, who grew up happily on the estate, where their mother ran a small herd of pedigree Guernsey cattle.

This was the 1920s and country living was still quite primitive. There was no electricity and water was pumped from a well 200 yards from the house. The old pump was eccentric and unpredictable, requiring 200 strokes a day to meet the family's needs provided you could get it to work at all. Thus, *water pump duty* was not the most popular chore.

Father Gavin was running a small engineering business from the wonder workshop and, with astute advertising in the equivalent of a DIY magazine, it grew to the extent that he decided he needed to establish a proper firm. The wilds of West Berkshire, he resolved, were clearly not the most appropriate place for this so he bought a property in North London.

Much of his work came from 'impecunious' inventors, from whom he would rarely, if ever, make money but he loved the challenge and excitement of innovation. Despite the penniless circumstances of a significant number of his clients, he somehow managed to extract enough profit to make his business viable and it continued its slow but steady growth.

Gavin knew the capital well and the move suited his business but he and his family were happy out in the country so he decided not to uproot them – opting instead for a daily commute of 60 miles a day from the local railway station at Kintbury. This was a decision his children were to appreciate forever, for they dearly loved the country life.

Nicholas's mother (maiden name Evelyn Winifred Alphega Mahon) was the daughter of a peppery senior officer in the

Indian Army. Major General Reginald Mahon did not take kindly to children, hence his daughter's unusual third Christian name: Alphega, being short for Alpha and Omega: the first and the last. She was, not surprisingly, an only child.

The Major General himself had been born into a military family in 1859 and married the daughter of a Lieutenant General Chamier. It is not known if she had been *his* first and last child. Most of Major General Mahon's military service was in India but, at the age of 40, he also served in South Africa during the Boer War, taking part in the siege of Ladysmith (in which the Boers laid siege to 5,500 British troops from November 2nd 1889 to February 27th 1900) being mentioned in despatches and awarded a Brevet Lieutenant-Colonelcy[1] in recognition of his service.

His distinguished career continued when he was made Director of the Ordnance Department in India in 1906 and he was awarded the Companionship of the Bath in 1907 and Companionship of the Star of India in 1911. He retired in 1911 but when World War 1 broke out in 1914 he was attached to the War Office in London and in 1915 he was sent to Canada and the United States on a 'special mission.'

After the war, Major General Mahon retired to Barton Holt at Kintbury, from where he combined business interests, such as the deputy chairmanship of the Calcutta Electrical Supply Corporation, with writing books. He became the author of several worthy tomes, including *The Indictment of Mary Queen of Scots.*

Barton Holt, rented from the Sutton Estate, was just a mile or two from the Goodharts' home. It was an imposing old

---

[1] A *brevet* referred to a warrant authorising a commissioned officer to hold a higher rank temporarily.

house, set back from the road and enclosed by a forbidding six-foot high fence. The interior was stuffed with fascinating relics brought back from India by Major General Mahon. The fire-place was a huge wooden carving and mysterious stringed musical instruments covered the walls. The hall was dominated by an elaborately carved wooden over-mantle decorated with figures and connected to the bedrooms by a long, wide and beautifully polished banister, which, provided their grandfa-ther was well and safely out of sight, was perfect for the Goodhart children to slide down at speed until they hit the square on top of the final pillar. The colourful drawing room had French windows looking out over splendid gardens, through which flowed the River Kennet – a source of joy to the grandchildren.

Attached to the house was a large aviary in which Grand-mother Mahon kept scores of beautiful canaries. Nicholas's sister Anstace would creep into the aviary in the hope that a bird would deposit a dropping on her head for that, she be-lieved, would bring her good luck.

Grandmother Mahon was a gregarious lady who was a regu-lar churchgoer and loved to mingle and chat with her numerous friends – among them Lord Burnham, who lived opposite at Barton Court. He was the Minister for Education and chaired the committee that created the *Burnham Scale* (a national pay scale for teachers).

Due, no doubt, to his transparent dislike of offspring, the Goodhart children had little affection for their distinguished grandfather, to whom they referred always as 'Grumpy', and that suited him very nicely for he had no time whatsoever for them. This mattered not one jot to the youngsters, who were enjoying such a happy childhood in their own home.

Nicholas's sister Anstace, who still lives in Kintbury, recalls:

'They were such happy, simple times. As a younger sister I hero-worshipped Nicholas and as an avid reader of the *William* books by Richmal Crompton, I tended to identify him with William, enjoying his minor misdemeanours as much as his successes.

'Nicholas was a shy boy and he hated the telephone. I vividly remember him lying, kicking and screaming, at the top of the stairs shouting that he would NOT ring up his grandmother to thank her for a present.

'Our Rover car had a very capacious box, outside at the back. Nicholas would hide in it when it was driven to Kintbury and the fun was to suddenly push open the lid and make faces at the passers-by. He also liked flattening pennies on the railway line.

'There was quite a large lake by our house and fishing was taken seriously. I can still see Nicholas standing at the end of the diving board proudly holding an enormous 13lb pike – I don't think a bigger fish has ever been caught there since. Setting night lines for eels was great fun too and quite a lot were caught, but these were not appreciated in the kitchen as during skinning they would wriggle and squirm even though their heads had been cut off.'

Schooling for all the Goodhart children started at five. They were sent to a small kindergarten in Kintbury to which they walked the two miles each way, come rain, hail or snow. The school was run by two spinster ladies, the Misses White, who provided a superb grounding in reading, writing and arithmetic. Their teaching methods were simple but effective. The children learned their twelve times tables and the arcane arts of multiplication and long division. Decimals would have been a step too far. Indeed, 'ordinary' people did not do decimals at all, but depended on quite complex tables of weights and measures, which provided sub-division down to a level beyond which, it was considered, you did not need to go. For example, area measurement – which the children learned off by heart – went:

144 square inches = 1 square foot
9 square feet = 1 square yard
30¼ square yards = 1 rod, pole or perch
40 rod, pole or perch = 1 rood
4 rood = 1 acre
640 acres = 1 square mile

Writing was taught very simply by means of a copy book. This had 26 pages, one for each letter of the alphabet. Across the top of each page there was a short phrase, such as *Patience is a virtue*, written in perfect copperplate, so that the book covered all upper and lower cases and examples of how various letters were joined up. Underneath each example were three lines and pupils slowly worked through the book, making three exact copies of the phrase at the top. This was all done with a pencil – ink being disallowed because it was far too messy.

Reading, in which the Goodhart children had received a good grounding from a succession of governesses, was a matter of learning spelling and how phrases were put together.

After kindergarten, the next stage of education for the Goodhart boys meant curtailment of the pastoral pleasures and parental care of life on the family estate. At eight years old they were each sent away to board at preparatory school, where they would spend four years before taking the Public School entrance examination. In May 1928 Nicholas was duly dispatched to Connaught House in Weymouth, where his two elder brothers were already ensconced.

Despite the presence of siblings to show him the ropes, boarding school was, at first, a gruelling experience for the very small and shy young Nicholas. He had grown up in a totally sheltered, comforting environment. Now he was suddenly thrown into an alien and disturbing outside world in which he cried himself to sleep for several nights. But he found his feet, began to enjoy it and started to make friends. He was a very intelligent boy and found classes easy. He didn't have to work hard and that helped enormously in the building of friendships because his peers frowned heavily upon 'swotting'.

The headmaster of Connaught House, Mr French ('Frenchie' to the boys) ruled his domain very firmly, with the aid of a cane. He was a linguist and, fittingly, taught French very successfully. Nicholas enjoyed that. From 'Frenchie' he not only acquired a thorough grounding in the language but an affinity with France and for the rest of his life it remained very much his favourite country.

He found English and History extremely dull and boring but in stark contrast was so fascinated by the numeracy subjects – Maths, Algebra and Geometry – that he could hardly wait for the next lesson.

Sport was very different. The 'bilious' boy dreaded every session, but he did take to roller-skating. The school had a gentle slope, leading to the gymnasium, down which the boys could skate, then whizz around the gym. He liked that a lot.

For Nicholas, there were no parental visits during the terms. Some pupils' homes were sufficiently close to take advantage of 'time out' from Saturday lunch time until Sunday evening, which was allowed at half term, but for young Goodhart's parents the journey would have been impractical, so his contact with home was restricted to the Sunday ritual of writing letters, which had to be approved by the duty master.

How he looked forward to the 13 weeks of holiday, when hunting rabbits and other game for the family larder was high on the list of enjoyable rural pursuits. The game larder was a large wooden framed box on legs, kept outdoors and covered with perforated zinc, in which the game so proudly gathered by the boys would be hung until considered ready for eating.

Another important and equally enjoyable use of holiday time was learning to drive. From the age of ten, the Goodhart boys were allowed to teach themselves to drive in an old car that was kept in one of the barns. Starting the engine, steering and braking were all straightforward enough, but gear changing was not. Gearboxes were known as 'crash', which meant that the cogs you wished to put into mesh with each other in order to change gear had to be going at the right speed before you tried to push them together. Failure in this process led to a loud grinding of metal which announced your incompetence to all and sundry in the vicinity and was the signal for merciless mockery. The necessary synchronism for avoidance of this humiliation was known as *double de-clutching*. Master this and you could drive; fail and you could not.

In the absence of mains services on the estate, light for the ground floor reception rooms of the house was provided by its own acetylene gas making plant. Beyond that, it was candle-light. A maid put out candlesticks every night and you simply took one of them as you went to bed.

Gavin Goodhart was delighted that his boys were showing an aptitude for engineering. When he decided to add the feature of a small lake to the front of the house, he built a 16-foot high dam across the valley so that he could plan a 12-foot diameter overshot waterwheel. He bought the bits and pieces for this and stood watching proudly as Kit and Nicholas assembled it under his supervision.

When, in 1930, he decided that they should have electricity, the job of wiring the house also fell to the boys – a task not quite so daunting as it sounds, since there was only one pendant per room, very few plug sockets and all the wiring was simply tacked to the walls. Basic though it was, the boys' wiring saw both their parents through to the end of their lives, Maman (as they called her) having lived six months beyond her 100th birthday before she died in 1989.

During one school holiday, 12-year-old Nicholas was summoned formally to his father's study and went in trepidation, imagining some severe reprimand, but when he got there, his father said simply, 'Now, what am I going to do with you?'

By which he meant, 'Which Public School am I going to send you to?'

Nicholas had assumed it would be Oundle, near Peterborough, maintained by the Worshipful Company of Grocers and sporting the Grocers' allegedly flatulent camel on its school badge. Oundle was very much engineering-oriented. His brother Kit was already there and, both having inherited their father's engineering gene, it had seemed the natural choice. But this was at the height of severe recession and Gavin Goodhart's business, Research Engineering, so indulgent of impecunious inventors, was having a hard time. Money was extremely tight and having two sons at Oundle simultaneously would cost a great deal.

Nicholas's eldest brother Tony was at the significantly less expensive Dartmouth Naval College and his father was well pleased with the numerical nature of the teaching and the relegation of the classics to a very minor role. Kit, it had been resolved, was to succeed his father at Research Engineering and he did not think that both should follow him into the firm.

So that was that. Gavin Goodhart told his youngest son: 'You had better go to Dartmouth. It's cheaper.'

Thus was the future of Nicholas Goodhart sealed for the next 40 years. He had no aptitude for a military career and no suitable characteristics; in fact, rather the reverse. But the

Royal Navy it was to be, via Dartmouth, elite training establishment for budding Naval officers.

The entry exam into Dartmouth College was no stern test for young Nicholas Goodhart. He found it easy and in next to no time he was in London, being taken to famous military outfitters Gieves to get his uniform. The world of bespoke tailoring was completely unknown to him, but the experienced tailors knew exactly what was required and coped well with the 'young gentleman.' There was one tricky point when it came to asking which side he dressed. To a boy whose voice was still two years away from breaking, the question was academic to the point of being utterly meaningless, but without too much embarrassment to either side, they reached some sort of conclusion, which enabled them to cut the cloth appropriately.

And so, resplendent in a shiny new uniform with a very unfamiliar cap, Nicholas stood on Paddington Station, waiting to board a train with other new cadets for the journey to Kingswear in Devon, there to cross the River Dart by ferry. Porters had taken charge of his luggage, which he would not see again until he got to the dormitory in Dartmouth College. 'Gentlemen', he learned, did not carry anything.

Thus began a steep learning curve, rich in fascination and interest. There was a lot of engineering – which was right up his street – and in the summer term there was dinghy racing and much messing about on the river in small boats. There was one lovely 35-ton yacht, which only the very senior were allowed to take out, but they needed crew, so he soon managed to get involved with that, too. And all instead of cricket. Pure bliss!

The only downside to this stimulating new life for young Goodhart was having to cope with a more or less permanent headache and feeling constantly 'a degree or two under'. Given that handicap, the winter and spring terms were considerably less enjoyable with obligatory football in the winter and rugby in the spring. Pure purgatory! By the end of every game he had a throbbing headache and if he was not being sick he was feeling sick.

The saving grace for Nicholas were the daily classes, which he enjoyed immensely, as he did the ceremonial parading and marching to the excellent band, made up of retired sailors and marines who, when they were not playing, looked after the 'young gentlemen' – waiting on table at meals, cleaning and polishing and making their beds.

Incongruous alongside that pampering was the severe discipline to which the cadets were subjected. They were regulated by Cadet Captains, whose job was to keep them in order and to motivate them to be the 'best term'. This they did by criticising all aspects of the cadets' activities, such as the number of minutes taken to dress, four being the limit, and enforcing the obligatory plunge into a freezing cold saltwater bath every morning.

At lights out, young Nicholas and the rest of the budding officers lay in bed shivering with horrid dread while the Cadet Captains told them how badly they were performing while, where deemed necessary, 'correcting' any shortcomings by use of the cane. Rather excessively, the 'young gentlemen' thought.

Such treatment could be tempered by the pleasures to be enjoyed in the canteen, where fourpence bought you the glorious treat of a fried egg on fried bread with a generous helping of beans. However, the cadets' total weekly pay was only one shilling (5p) and that had to pay for all outgoings, so the *fried egg special* was only an occasional delight.

It is hard to believe, in today's very much softer and politically correct society, that the 'young gentlemen' being put through all Dartmouth's character-forming ordeals were as young as twelve or thirteen and Nicholas's sister Anstace tells a delightful little story which makes that point very well:

> 'Nicholas was home on leave from his first term at Dartmouth and we were invited to a big children's Christmas party at which there were lots of games and other entertainment. He was in his Naval uniform and, being shy, was hating every minute of the party, but the final straw was when he was asked to take part in *Ring-a-ring-o-roses,* whereupon he pulled himself up to his full height (which was not very much, because at 13 he was still rather small) and announced:
>
> "Members of the King's Navy do NOT play *Ring-a-ring-o-roses!*"'

Without ever having to stretch himself, Nicholas remained at the top of the academic tree throughout his time at Dartmouth. In their last year, the brightest cadets joined the Alpha class, members of which were allowed to give up their least favourite subjects. Nicholas chose to give up History and English, which meant that, despite doing no swotting whatsoever, he was able to complete the passing out exams with ease and distinction.

In December 1936, 17-year-old Nicholas passed out from Dartmouth College. The very small boy had suddenly shot up to 6ft at the age of 16 and now cut a rather handsome figure with his light brown hair, fair complexion and very blue eyes – but his exceptional shyness remained. ('It meant I never looked anyone in the eye and means that, to this day, I do not recognise people and frequently have to be reminded who they are,' he said much later)

Now, it was time to move on to the next phase of his Royal Navy training...

The training cruiser HMS *Frobisher* was a traditional cruiser left over from World War One and on first joining the seagoing Navy all Naval Cadets did one cruise of two and a half months. Dartmouth cadets were joined by others whose education had been through more traditional public or grammar school routes and those from Dartmouth assumed an air of superiority, snobbish in their knowledge of Naval parlance and condescendingly calling the public school boys 'pubs'. This disdain was misplaced, however, because the newcomers merged quickly and by the end of the cruise there were no significant differences.

The main purpose of the *Frobisher* cruise was to enable the cadets to live as sailors and to discover what life was like for an ordinary seaman. The cruise serving this purpose for Nicholas was to the West Indies. They arrived on board very early in the morning of a bitterly cold day in January 1937. They were freezing but they soon discovered that one of the joys of steam ships was that they always had a boiler fired up to run the generator and serve other essential purposes and, consequently, were permanently warm.

The cadets were divided into groups and assigned to a mess. This consisted of a long wooden table about 3ft wide, sticking inboard from the side of the ship, on each side of which was a wooden bench the same length as the table. Overhead were a series of pairs of hooks about seven inches apart, each pair being 18 inches from the next. Each cadet had to sling his hammock between a pair of these hooks. There was also a line of lockers, in which they kept their gear.

When not being slept in, each hammock had to be lashed, along with the bed gear, into a tight sausage, which had to be stood on end in the *hammock nets*, a rectangular space with a vertical steel post at each corner and a strip of net surrounding the posts. It just about held the number of hammocks in that compartment – but only if they were lashed properly and standing correctly on end.

Feeding arrangements were, by normal standards, unusual. Every member of the mess had to take his turn as a cook. There were two cooks a day and they were excused all other duties during that time. They had a big billy can (a cylindrical tin can with a wire handle used for boiling water over a camp fire) and a plate, knife, fork, spoon and mug per person. Their job was to draw the day's rations from the victualling store, then to distribute it fairly between all members of the mess. The rations were basic dry goods – flour, bread, ship's biscuits, tea, sugar, some meat, potatoes and occasionally vegetables. There were no facilities in or near the mess so the duty cooks had to put together what they wanted and take it to a central galley, where it was cooked for them. Skills among the cooks of the mess were, to say the least, limited and the cadets' fare was predictable and unappetising... almost invariably a sort of stew and suet pudding.

Such deprivation was a minor matter, however, to the Dartmouth cadets, among whom young Nicholas continued to excel without really trying.

The next phase in his education was the Naval equivalent of university – the Royal Naval Engineering College at Keyham, Devonport – and that too was taken effortlessly in his stride.

The little village of Inkpen and the pastoral joys of the family estate continued to provide enjoyment and comfort when he was home on leave and for a teenager with a growing appetite for adventure, it could sometimes prove a surprisingly exciting place to be.

Every Easter, members of the Cambridge University Gliding Club took up residence in the nearby Vale of Pewsey for a week of hill-soaring. If the wind blew from the south or west the pilots concentrated their efforts on the line of hills at the other end of the valley but if, as often happened at that time of the year, it came more from the north, they set their sights on the slopes of Inkpen Beacon, an area of brooding hills and big skies just behind the Goodharts' home, which could be almost guaranteed to provide the right conditions for a memorable day's flying.

In 1938, the northerlies were particularly favourable. Day after day the Cambridge pilots flew their gliders towards the lift that they knew they would find on the hills a couple of miles behind the house and, day after day, 18-year-old Nicholas pedalled his old one-speed bike up to the beacon to join the small knot of people who gathered there to watch.

He was fascinated by the grace and beauty of those lovely machines as they slid effortlessly along the ridge, often only 10ft above his head, and a plan began to take shape in his head.

If they could do it, so could he.

His plan took an unexpected step forward when his parents, both as fascinated as he was by the gliders flying above their house, invited two of the pilots to tea. Young Nicholas made no secret of his interest and plied the pilots with so many questions that one of them gave him a copy of *Sailplane & Glider* magazine.

As he flicked through its pages, enthralled by the pictures and stories of men pitting their skills against nature, his eye was drawn to a small advertisement: *WANT TO BE A GLIDER PILOT?* He quickly noted that the dates mentioned in the advertisement coincided handily with his summer leave. *Yes,* he thought. *If other people could do it, so could he.* So *would* he. It was the start of an adventure that was to endure for 35 years.

Sutton Bank was the home of the Yorkshire Gliding Club, a hill site on the fringes of the North Yorkshire Moors, just a few miles north of the city of York itself. As Nicholas made his way up the steep and twisting road leading to it, he had little idea what he was in for.

He was a methodical young man, so he had done enough research to know that the Yorkshire Gliding Club was one of the best in the country and that its position on top of a 600-foot escarpment at the edge of the moors promised hours of supreme flying for those skilful enough to take advantage of it. But he had no way of knowing if he had what it took to learn to fly or if he would enjoy it even if he had.

The first signs were not promising.

He and his 15 fellow students were ushered towards an un-gainly contraption which, they were told, would either help them learn to fly or put them off the skies for ever. This, they were informed sternly, was the Dagling, a so-called 'primary glider' which was not, in fact, designed to fly in anything more than the most rudimentary fashion. The students would be learning to 'fly' while sitting in something not much more refined than a kitchen chair suspended from a tripod, with a crude wing sticking out on each side.

The machine would be manhandled into place, facing the wind, so that Nicholas and his new friends could experience the effect of the controls and learn how to move the stick to operate the ailerons in such a way that the wings were balanced. Once they had mastered that technique they would graduate to a few slides along the grass before, if they were successful, moving on to some controlled 'hops' across the ground.

The really talented, or brave, could quickly reach the dizzy heights of 10ft above the ground before descending swiftly back to earth in something that might only loosely be described as a landing. Only when the instructor was happy that they had learned those basics would they be invited to take the controls as the Dagling was launched optimistically into the sky by a bungee (a giant elastic band) pulled tight by their friends. It was a difficult and sometimes dangerous way to learn to fly but in those days – before the arrival of dual-controlled training gliders – there was no alternative.

Little wonder that, as the course progressed, more and more of the trainee pilots could be seen taking their meals standing up because their nether regions were so battered by repeated heavy landings on a seat that had neither suspension nor even cushion. Little wonder, either, that all but four of the original 16 students had given up long before the fortnight was over.

It was inevitable that someone as single-minded as Nicholas Goodhart would be one of the few to see the course through, no matter how bruised his backside and that, on the last day, with the necessary breeze blowing in gently from the west, he would be awarded his first gliding accolade – his 'C' badge to mark the fact that he had managed a 'flight' of five minutes.

Two of the other surviving candidates achieved the same distinction before the fourth – an attractive young lady named Forbes – spun into the ground after getting into a muddle with the controls and finished her five minute 'flight' sitting, embarrassed but unhurt, in the remains of a Dagling shattered almost beyond recognition.

She explained that she (like a lot of novice glider pilots) had mistakenly believed that she could gain height simply by pulling back on the stick to lift the glider's nose – an action which, in fact, has a result totally opposite to the one required, as the glider merely stalls and dives into the ground.

Young Nicholas left the scene knowing that he was lucky not to have been the one sitting in the smashed wreckage of the training glider – for he had thought precisely the same thing.

Having taken his first tentative steps towards becoming a glider pilot and with the enthusiasm first inspired by those fragile aircraft flying above his head on Inkpen Beacon still burning brightly, Nicholas was determined to push himself to the limit to see where his new hobby might take him. He was only 19 but already he was most emphatically not the sort of fellow to settle for second best.

While being away at college for most of the year was something of a hindrance as far as his flying career was concerned, he did at least have the holidays in which to make up for lost time. He spent as much of that time as he could at the Oxford University and City Gliding Club where, though conditions were never as favourable as those which had seen aircraft soaring for hours above the hills around the Vale of Pewsey, he was able to learn much more about the rudiments of the sport.

It was pure luck that had seen him choose a gliding club where training was in the hands of one of the truly great figures of the gliding world. Robert Kronfield was still only 34 but he had already gained legendary status among his peers. In 1929 he had been the first glider pilot to fly a distance of 100km (62.5 miles) and two years later had been the first to fly a glider both ways across the English Channel (a feat that won him £1,000 from the *Daily Mail*). He had gone on to set gliding world records for both distance (164km) and for height (2,589m) before, in 1933, fleeing his native Austria when Hitler's Nazi government banned Jews like him from flying. By 1938 he had settled in England and become chief instructor of the Oxford club, just in time for Nicholas to become one of his first pupils. Young Goodhart could not have had a better role model – as a pilot or as a human being – and it was beginning to look as if, for the boy from Inkpen, the sky really would be the limit as he completed his education and left Keyham in 1940, as a Lieutenant.

Meanwhile, that troublesome Adolf Hitler had been making his unwelcome presence felt across Europe and Britain was now at war with Germany.

3.   Goodhart at war

LIEUTENANT NICHOLAS GOODHART, 22, was soon to discover that travelling in wartime could have a surreal quality when, his engineering training having ended in December 1940, he was directed by Their Lordships of the Admiralty to take a train to Thurso, there to join his first ship – *HMS Formidable*. They sent him a First Class ticket for the purpose and he found himself on a train travelling north from Inverness.

It was late on New Year's Eve and the young officer could have been forgiven for thinking that the date would have no significance whatsoever. After all, there was a war on and such fripperies as welcoming in the New Year would surely be on hold. But this was Scotland and no jumped-up little Austrian with a silly black moustache was going to be permitted to interfere with such a serious business as Hogmanay.

Soon after leaving Inverness, the train pulled up at a small station. The driver and the fireman got out and were quickly joined by the guard. The fireman, carrying the customary lump of coal, led the way to the stationmaster's office, where he stepped ceremoniously over the threshold and presented the coal to the stationmaster.

The train's astonished passengers then looked on in envy as enormous tots of whisky were quickly poured and just as quickly downed, to be followed by repeated exchanges of traditional greetings before the ceremony concluded and the train's crew re-embarked to continue the journey.

It soon became apparent that this ritual, far from being a one-off event, was to be re-enacted at *every* wayside station – of which there were many. At each station passed, the train crew became visibly more unsteady and the wait became ever longer. There were around 500 sailors on board and it didn't take them long to cotton on to this 'first footing' and to join in with gusto. Finally, at 0600 hours, a bedraggled shambles of a train tottered with unabashed inebriety into Thurso and managed to stop half a mile from the station, having run out of steam, coal, water and motivation. *Happy New Year!*

And there was more insobriety to come. When Lieutenant Goodhart duly reported to the Senior Naval Officer, he told him that *Formidable* was not in Scapa Flow at present and that he should stay at the Thurso Hotel to await her reappearance. Having done so, he was recruited by the Senior Officer to take part in crucial activities such as shooting capercaillies, the large turkey-like game birds quite common in those parts. This involved Nicholas beating in the snow and the Senior Officer shooting – an exercise in which the capercaillies were the clear winners.

He then took him to visit the lighthouse at Dunnet Head, where the keepers, who rarely saw anybody at all, made their own whisky. No sooner had they arrived than the keepers were pressing large mugs of firewater into their guests' willing hands. A good time was had by all and friendship was well and truly cemented before the naval party made its way, happily but not without difficulty, back to Thurso.

After five days, a signal was received from the Admiralty in-structing Lieutenant Goodhart to return to his home in Southern England, there to await further instructions. These arrived three weeks after his original orders and required him to proceed to Swansea and join a vessel, which turned out to be a 10,000-ton Swedish collier loading coke for Port Sudan in the Red Sea.

Like many merchant ships of that time, other than the officers' quarters there were six cabins, which were used in peacetime by the owners and an occasional passenger. Somehow, the Admiralty had arranged that twelve men – six naval officers and six ENSA personnel – would be carried, two to a cabin. Quite how they stood with regard to the Geneva Convention was not clear. The ship had an enormous Swedish flag painted on each side amidships to emphasise her neutrality.

The tone for the whole voyage was set on the first night. Dinner was at 2000 hours sharp and all were standing behind their chairs awaiting the appearance of the Captain who, as soon as he came in, announced: 'Chentlemen, velcom to my ship. It is my birthday. Ve vill trink a leetle toast.'

The stewards, who were obviously ready for this, instantly poured *aquavit* (a strong, neat Scandinavian spirit) into the waiting wine glasses. These had to be downed in one gulp, with the British determined not to lose face by coughing as the alcohol burned its way down. Then they sat down as the shot glasses were refilled for the toasting ritual to be repeated many times as the Captain introduced other officers.

In a couple of days, loading was complete and they set sail for the Clyde, where a convoy was assembling. It was not long before 30 merchant ships set off in a generally north-westerly direction at 10 knots.

As the voyage progressed, dinner each night was completely formal and followed the same routine as that first night, the only difference being that the Captain's opening speech saluted someone else's birthday. From the first mate to the ship's cat, he was invariably able to find a birthday to justify the toasts.

The defence of this convoy was pitifully small, just one old destroyer and a couple of trawlers, but they managed not to lose any ships to submarines. Air attack was more effective and, at lunchtime on each of the first four days, German aircraft bombed the stragglers, sinking at least four ships. Fortunately for the vessel containing Nicholas Goodhart, the Germans did not like attacking the body of the convoy. Because all ships carried small arms, there was a danger of being shot down in a low attack and, being neutral, his ship was in the middle.

After four days, the convoy was out of range of air attacks and able to continue westward.

In due course, Goodhart's ship approached 23° West and the Captain announced that they would now leave the convoy. Asked why, he showed them a chart of the Atlantic with a big red line down 23°W. On the west side of the line there was a big red *11* and on the east side there was a big red *111*.

'Chentlemen,' he said, 'on this side, because it is so dangerous, we get three times our pay and on the other side we get only two times.'

His logic was irrefutable. They turned and followed the line south, down to about 35°N, at which point both the line and the ship turned south-eastward until they reached the Moroccan coast. The sadness on board was palpable when they could go no further and had, reluctantly, to cross into 'two times' waters.

A few nights later, when the Captain came in to dinner, it was clear that he had already had a drink or two as he announced, without delay: 'Tonight, Chentlemen, it really *is* my birthday!'

This was the signal for the start of an incredibly drunken evening, involving officers, passengers and crew alike. Within three hours, everybody was drunk. Most just lay, hopelessly, helplessly where they fell – in the scuppers, the passages, wherever.

Goodhart, who was just short of total incapacitation, was able to struggle up the ladders to the unlit bridge, where he found not a soul – no lookouts, no officer of the watch, no sign whatsoever of human existence. The ship was on autopilot, chugging along at her usual 10 knots, on a calm tropical sea, lit only by a weak moonlight.

As Goodhart's eyes became accustomed to that light, he began to make out the hazy outline of another unlit vessel crossing them ahead from port to starboard. The 'rule of the road' puts the onus of avoidance of collision on the ship which has the other on its starboard side, so he took a vague bearing, then watched, expecting it to take avoiding action. But, as the two ships closed in on each other, it became apparent that no effort was being made by the approaching vessel to change its course.

Collision now looked inevitable and Goodhart, in his befuddled state, could only watch with increasing concern. It was a close run thing. The other ship's stern cleared their bows by no more than 200 yards. They had been 35 seconds from disaster – and he was the only one on board who had witnessed the drama. No point in seeking corroboration of his story, however. He was almost as drunk as everybody else – so who would believe him?

A couple of days later, the ship's carpenter was seen to be very and somewhat furtively busy. He had already rigged up a swimming pool, made from hatch covers and a tarpaulin which (in days long before the advent of air-conditioning) was much used and appreciated by all on board. 'Chippy' was now building a platform over the pool on which a chair was arranged so that, at the pull of a lever, it would tip over backwards, hurtling anyone unfortunate enough to be sitting in it upside down into the water. Suspicious though this construction appeared, none of the passengers had a clue what it was all about.

At dinner the following night, the Captain announced that the next day the ship would be crossing the equator and that all the passengers were required to assemble on the foredeck adjacent to the pool at 1130 hours. This they dutifully did – to find the bosun dressed as an extremely fierce-looking King Neptune, equipped with an enormous open razor and accompanied by a band of piratical ruffians bearing buckets of shaving foam and paintbrushes.

The passengers, by now growing increasingly anxious and realising that the paint brushes were intended for application of the foam, were mightily relieved to note that King Neptune's huge razor was made of wood. It didn't take them long, either, to work out that further ruffians in the pool were there to manhandle anyone unfortunate enough to find themselves deposited in the water and the purpose of 'Chippy's mysterious platform construction was suddenly and alarmingly apparent.

Much declaiming in Swedish established that all those who did not have a crossing-the-line certificate (which, of course, meant *all* the passengers) had to be 'initiated'. One after another, the passengers were seized by the pirates, hoisted on to the platform and unceremoniously restrained in the chair while shaving foam was daubed liberally over various parts of the anatomy and King Neptune got to work with his razor.

Woe betide any passenger reckless enough to open his mouth in protest, for a brush full of foam would be instantly thrust in. At the appropriate moment, the lever was tripped and the ruffians in the pool seized each hapless initiate and held him under to ensure that he really understood King Neptune's domain. Finally, to compensate for their ordeal, each passenger was presented with a handwritten certificate, sewn onto a piece of canvas, confirming that he had been well and truly initiated.

In due course the ship went into Cape Town for 24 hours, to refuel and re-provision, thus providing an opportunity for passengers and crew to have a run ashore. Goodhart was forced to miss that long-awaited pleasure because he was suffering a terrible migraine but, when recovered, he was pleased to note that the range and quality of food on board had been greatly improved – though it remained secondary to alcohol, which still held pride of place.

The voyage up the East African coast was uneventful and (56 days and 13,200 nautical miles out from Glasgow) they reached Port Sudan in the Red Sea, only to be told that all jetties were occupied and they would have to anchor off until there was a slot. The passengers hoped this might provide an opportunity for some sea-swimming, until they realised that the water was teeming with sharks. The crew ran a strong line through a block hanging from a davit, with a large meat hook on the end, produced a distinctly unpleasant old hunk of meat for bait and, within minutes, were hoisting an enormous shark aboard.

The ship's cook, who was Chinese, then appeared with a large knife and hacked off the dorsal fin, while firmly refusing any other bits of the creature, which was dumped over the side. Immediately, the water became a foaming red mess as the shark's mates tore its corpse apart – thus confirming that this was no place for a swim. But Goodhart recorded that the shark's fin soup they had for dinner that night was 'excellent'.

A couple of days later the coaling wharf was clear and, as soon as the ship was secured, Goodhart and Co went ashore to try to find somebody who could tell them what to do next. Eventually, they succeeded in unearthing an honorary consul-type, who was able to contact the British embassy where they, in turn, contacted the naval authority which, they were quite relieved to discover, actually knew of their existence and arranged for them to be given train tickets to Alexandria.

After a relatively simple journey, with an overnight stop in Cairo, they arrived in Alexandria – to find that the various ships they were supposed to be joining were not there. There was much secrecy, but they managed to establish that there was a reasonable probability that the missing vessels would be returning to Alexandria in the not too distant future.

It turned out that they were up in the Greek Peloponnese, pursuing the Italian fleet and engaging them with great success off Cape Matapan. Goodhart and his fellow travellers didn't know it at the time, but this was the swansong of the Italian Fleet in the Mediterranean. What was left of it (it had lost three 8-inch cruisers, two smaller cruisers and two destroyers and suffered severe damage to a battleship) retired to the 'safety' of its home port at Taranto where, eight months later, a strike from *HMS Illustrious* demonstrated the illusory nature of that 'safety' by torpedoing three battleships and two cruisers and sinking two other ships.

On 2nd April 1941 the victorious British ships were back in Alexandria and Goodhart was at last able to join HMS *Formidable* and begin to put into practice what he had trained so long for. It was hard work and, with extreme heat in the machinery spaces, debilitating. Air conditioning did not exist. All that could be done was to provide a ventilation system with large fans able to refresh the compartments with cooler outside air at frequent intervals.

Despite the ventilation system, cases of heatstroke were common, since the temperature in many compartments, particularly in machinery spaces, remained far too high. There was a simple cure for the resultant heatstroke; victims were laid out on deck while a water hose was played over their bodies. Prevention could be achieved by taking enough salt to replace that lost through sweating and large billy cans containing a brew made from salt, lime juice and barley were hung up so that everybody could try to maintain their salt levels.

Towards the end of May, *Formidable* was on the way to Crete to assist in the evacuation of Allied troops from the island when she was hit by two 1,000lb bombs from German Stukas, blowing a huge hole in her starboard side just above the water-line.

Unlike their American cousins, British aircraft carriers had an armoured flight deck protecting all the important com-partments in the ship. However, both forward and aft, the compartments were mostly living spaces, which were unoccu-pied when the ship was in action, hence they had no armour protection. Of the two bombs that hit the ship, one hit the armour and bounced over the side but the other penetrated the living spaces, blowing a hole (30ft by 25ft) in the starboard bow stretching down to the water line. This seriously limited the speed of the ship because the bow wave came inboard, impact-ing on the forward facing bulkheads.

The safe speed meant an extremely slow return to Alexan-dria, where to Goodhart fell the task of organising a temporary repair with a patch. Though he didn't know it at the time, it had been arranged that the US Navy would fully repair the ship in their dockyard in Norfolk, Virginia.

Temporary repair effected, *Formidable* sailed through the Suez Canal and round Africa to Norfolk. The Western half of the Mediterranean was under German/Italian control, making it necessary to exit the Mediterranean via the Canal and pro-ceed to Norfolk via the Cape of Good Hope, which meant that the patched-up ship was exposed to tropical storms in the Southern Ocean, but despite some rather alarming flexing, Goodhart's patch held firm.

In October 1941, Goodhart was appointed to HMS *Dido,* which was also under repair in the USA at the Brooklyn Navy Yard. On December 7th – the day the Japanese bombed Pearl Harbour, thus igniting the USA's entry into the war – *Dido* sailed from Brooklyn to the Mediterranean.

Goodhart's Christmas was to be in Malta – but most of his time was spent in the caves under Valetta because the island was being bombed remorselessly.

The Grand Harbour in Malta, a deep cleft in the rock structure, contained sufficient jetties to accommodate the capital ships of the entire pre-war Mediterranean Fleet. Leading off the jetties there are extensive caves and, since Goodhart and the rest were spending Christmas there, they made the best of it, setting up camp in the first class air-raid shelter that the caves provided.

Due to its proximity to Italy, Malta was under almost continuous air attack. At this stage the air defence consisted of just three Gloster Gladiators – known forever afterwards as *Faith, Hope* and *Charity* – a trio of outdated biplanes which, against all odds, proved sufficient deterrent to safeguard the island from invasion. The Italian/German air capability was able, however, effectively to deny Allied shipping access to the island throughout 1941.

In June of that year, 17 merchant ships with strong Naval escorts set off from Gibraltar and Alexandria but only two reached the island and one of those was sinking and only just succeeded in beaching. A second attempt was made in 1942, on which occasion *Dido* was part of the Naval escorting force.

Five out of 14 managed to get through with the loss of two cruisers. The Captain of *Dido* had taken the trouble to study the German dive-bombing technique and discovered that it involved lining up on the ship's wake to start the dive and pulling through on the line, releasing the bomb at the point indicated by the bombsight. Thus, he realised that the attack depended totally on the ship maintaining its course. His solution, as seen from the engine room (Goodhart's action station) went as follows:

Dido's ten 5.25 inch anti-aircraft guns[2] would start banging away, followed by the Bofors 40mm machine guns, which indicated that the bombers had entered their dive.

There were always four aircraft in the line and Dido's Captain would wait until all four had entered the dive. Suddenly, the engine room telegraphs would jangle with the instruction 'Stop port, full-ahead starboard,' or vice-versa.

The engines were controlled by large steam valves, which had equally large hand-wheels that were double-manned so that the Captain got what he ordered in the shortest possible time. Goodhart and the rest would see the rudder tell-tale go hard over and the ship would roll outboard while executing a maximum rate turn.

Down below decks, this was the interesting moment as a few seconds later there would be an enormous *Thump!* as the bomb went off on the original course line of the ship. The only effect was that all the lights went out (no problem because the emergency lights came on automatically) and in the machinery spaces the air was filled with asbestos dust shaken out of the steam pipe lagging.

---

[2] In theory these were able to hit aircraft at 40,000 feet but in practice had never actually hit one – but since the aircraft had never actually hit Dido either, the score was a mutually satisfactory goal-less draw.

Other cruisers came out to replace those that were dive-bombed and sunk and were then themselves sunk – but *Dido* just kept on and on. It remained a mystery to Nicholas Goodhart why his Captain didn't explain to the others how they could spoil the fun of the dive-bombers.

Goodhart's war 'score' for 1941 had been: five months cruising, five months enjoying life in the States and two months on operations. 'Not bad,' he figured.

In July 1942 Goodhart was loaned to HMS *Aldenham* as Chief Engineer Officer – a temporary replacement for an officer who had gone sick. But in September he returned to HMS *Dido*, serving as an engineer officer watch-keeper, as the ship continued activity in the Eastern Mediterranean.

Dido then operated out of Bone in North Africa, supporting the successful allied landing in Sicily. When Palermo was secured, she was ordered to move and operate from there, as the Allies continued their advance up the Italian Peninsula.

There were still pockets of resistance in Sicily and, on her way to Palermo, she was instructed to carry out a bombardment of Marsala – an event which Goodhart, with typical understatement, was later to describe thus:

> 'It took no more than half-an-hour to lob a number of shells in the general direction of the town as we went by and early the next day we anchored at Palermo. As far as we engineers were concerned it had been an entirely uneventful trip.'

Late in 1943, as the Allies were pushing the Germans northwards on the Italian mainland, it was decreed that the landing craft which had been used first in the North African landings and then in Operation *Husky* to secure Sicily, were no longer needed in the Mediterranean but would be needed back in the

UK early in 1944 to prepare for Operation *Overlord* (the long-awaited Allied invasion of Normandy in June 1944).

Thus it came about that, in November 1943, a convoy of 28 LCT (Landing Craft Tank) vessels set off from Gibraltar with one trawler as escort. It was realised that the Royal Naval Volunteer Reserve officers who ran these ships were not qualified in open ocean navigation so, in the particular case of LCT 403, a young Royal Navy Lieutenant H.D. Howse, a navigator, was put in temporary command for the voyage.

On the day before the convoy sailed, he had run into Lieutenant Goodhart, an old friend and team-mate from Dartmouth College days, who had been instructed to return to the UK and report to the Admiralty. Goodhart had been in Gibraltar for several days trying, without success, to find a way of returning to the UK. He had tried the airport, only to be told that even Air Marshals had to wait for three weeks and getting a berth in a troop carrier at short notice was even more difficult.

So when Lieutenant Howse suggested that he should join LCT 403 as a supernumerary, Goodhart accepted with alacrity.

Normally, the crew of LCT 403 was entirely RNVR so, at first, there were some differences of opinion over their way of running a ship compared with that of the RN, but this was sorted out (at least temporarily) and the convoy departed Gibraltar in some semblance of order and headed out into the Atlantic, where one of the extremely efficient Lieutenant Howse's first requests was for the deviation card for the compass. This produced a blank look from the RNVR: 'Deviation card?'

'Yes, you know. The table showing the compass error on various headings.'

'Ah, yes. But, oh no. We don't have one because the compass always points towards the vehicles when they are embarked.'

It was an exchange which resulted in the near collapse of the efficient young RN officer! So they set about constructing a deviation card by taking the sun's true bearing at sunrise and sunset and employing other clever navigational tricks – all of which depended, however, on knowing what time it was.

The ship had neither radio nor chronometer and the only source of time was a deckwatch. This was checked every day by means of a signal from the escorting trawler which, at five minutes before noon, hoisted one black ball then, at noon precisely, hauled it back down again. On LCT 403, they wrote down the reading on their deckwatch so that after three or four days they knew not only the error but also the rate at which it was increasing.

There was one other important signal from the trawler. Sometime during the forenoon each day, a set of signal flags would go up which, after studying the code book for a while, Goodhart & Co discovered meant 'stop, change valve springs'.

This particular type of LCT was driven by two petrol engines with exposed overhead valve gear. Clearly, the manufacturers knew a thing or two, because each valve had two springs, one inside the other, so that one broken spring (a not infrequent occurrence) did not matter.

As soon as the signal was made, the entire convoy stopped and the engine-room team of a petty officer and a stoker (plus Goodhart) rushed below and worked along the lines of valves, looking for broken springs. Putting on a new valve spring was, given the right tool, not difficult, but there was one critical snag. On no account was the valve to be allowed to escape, because it would drop immediately into the cylinder and then there was no alternative but to take the cylinder head off. Instead of taking five minutes, the job would then take five hours!

On completion of the inspection and any necessary spring changes, each LCT hoisted the affirmative and, after twenty minutes or so, even though there might not be a full house of affirmatives, a signal hoist would go up in the trawler, indicating that they should prepare to get under way again. At the haul-down, off they went – except, perhaps, for one or two who had committed the cardinal error.

By this time, they were getting sufficiently far north to be in range of Luftwaffe Junkers 88s based in France, which would turn up around lunch-time and strafe them. Goodhart's vessel had two Lewis guns with which they shot back until honour was satisfied and the result was another entirely acceptable no-score draw.

Since the role of an LCT was to run ashore on a shallow beach, where the vehicles they carried could drive off without drowning, they were built not unlike large punts and drew only about 3 feet at the stern and even less at the bows. It was a design that was less than ideal in the open ocean, as Goodhart & Co were soon to discover when, on the seventh day, a severe storm blew up from the southwest and by dawn they were on their own.

They had no idea where the rest of the convoy was, or even if it still existed. Alone like this, station keeping on a dark night was, to say the least, not easy. This left them with two major problems – to keep the vessel afloat and to navigate to their official destination of Milford Haven.

Priority had to be given to keeping the vessel afloat. The first lick of water that came over the side split the canvas cover over the vehicle hold from end to end and it promptly blew away. This left them in real danger of sinking as more water came over the side and the hold began to fill. There was a bilge pump but the sump from which it took its suction quickly blocked up with rubbish. The sump was close to the bottom of the iron ladder on the after bulkhead so it was, in theory, only a matter of shinning down the ladder and clearing the sump. But – and it was a very *big* but – the hold by this time had a lot of water in it, sloshing from end to end as the ship pitched.

Had it been just water, all would have been well, but it included all the inevitable clutter which had been stored in the hold – baulks of timber, luggage, tables, packing cases, 40-gallon drums, spare gear, chairs, ropes, etc – all rumbling back and forth and hitting the after bulkhead with considerable force.

With typical understatement, many years later, Nicholas Goodhart described it thus:

> 'We found ourselves playing 'chicken' up and down the ladder, trying to keep the suction clear. It behoved one not to miss one's footing.'

A man more given to hyperbole might have described it as a desperate struggle to stay alive while trying to prevent the vessel from sinking.

As time went by, the wind veered steadily and as it veered it created increasing problems for LCT 403. With the wind on the beam, navigation became even more difficult. They knew which way they were heading but they did not know which way they were going! All they knew was that it was undoubtedly sideways, but by how much? Was it 10 degrees? 15 maybe? Perhaps as much as 20? And it was towards France, where they definitely did not want to be going.

It had been darkly overcast ever since the storm blew up and it was becoming increasingly important to know where they were when, at about midnight, conditions suddenly cleared, providing – as the moon was very nearly full – enough of a horizon, whenever they were on the crest of a wave, to make it worth trying to take some star sights.

Goodhart set about doing this – though it was hardly the job of an engineer – and had just finished taking six stars when an enormous wave descended vertically on the little bridge, carrying away the sextant, the sextant box and the deckwatch, as well as the two lockers on the after bulkhead of the bridge structure, which contained all the food. Fortunately, none of the men was swept overboard, everybody on the bridge managed to hold on and the sailor who had been writing down the sextant and deckwatch readings heroically held on to the piece of paper he was using.

To everybody's surprise and Goodhart's astonishment, the sights, when worked out, established a good cocked hat[3] and at last they knew where they were to within about eight miles.

At this point, a new problem began to emerge. It was well known that you should never drive an LCT head on into a heavy sea because it would climb up one side of a wave and, on reaching the crest, would bang heavily down on its flat bottom on the other side. This banging was known to cause structural failure at the after end of the vehicle hold. As the wind continued to veer towards the north, it became necessary for LCT 403 to be steered progressively more to the east, which, coupled with the drift, was certainly not the direction in which they wanted to go. Reaching Milford Haven was clearly not on, but

---

[3] In those days, navigation was a complex process involving a lot of time and mathematics to draw a line on your chart somewhere along which you believed your position lay. There were various possible sources of information and each provided a position line. By selecting suitable sources intersecting position lines could be produced. If you had three position lines these would enclose a triangle which was called a 'cocked hat' – the assumption being that your position lay somewhere in the cocked hat. By extension, a cocked hat is the area enclosed within any group of position lines.

on the tenth day they were more than delighted to see Bishop Rock and decided to try for Falmouth instead.

They knew the petrol tanks were leaking and salt water was getting in but there was nothing they could do about that except to hope that the salt water would not rise as high as the pipe feeding the engines. Also, they did not dare to stop the engine to look at the valve springs because this was, most emphatically, not the sort of sea in which to drift out of control. A Coastal Command Liberator[4] had circled them at one stage and, although communication by Aldis lamp (used for passing messages using Morse code) had been inconclusive, at least now someone knew they still existed and might turn up to help somewhere.

Once past The Lizard, the sea eased considerably and they were able to reach Falmouth, where their incredible journey had a fittingly dramatic finale. As he brought LCT 403 alongside the jetty, Lieutenant Howse called for 'engines full-astern', to take the way off the ship (i.e. stop its forward motion through the water) but at precisely that instant both engines spluttered to a standstill because salt water had finally worked its way into the fuel lines.

They hit the end of the jetty with an almighty crunch!

The ship's company stepped ashore with a collective sigh of relief and a firm conviction that they had done their bit as regards LCT 403 and it was now somebody else's problem.

---

[4] During World War Two, RAF Coastal Command operated a number of US-built B-24 'Liberator' aircraft configured in an anti-submarine role. The B-24 was designed for and much used in a conventional bombing role but these customised aircraft were supplied to the UK under Lend/Lease for use in the South West Approaches. They were much feared by German U-boat captains.

Goodhart, meanwhile, was left to ponder whether it might have been wiser to have hitched a lift from Gibraltar in some other type of craft.

In January 1944, with the Allied victory in Europe now just a few months away, Lieutenant Nicholas Goodhart's military career took a new turn. The specialist training of engineer officers had consisted of 11 terms of marine engineering at the Royal Naval Engineering College, Keyham, Devonport, which moved to Manadon, on the outskirts of Plymouth, and began to include some Air Engineering. Goodhart did a two-week course there to add Air Engineering to his qualifications – but far more important than that was the decision that all who could pass the medical should become qualified pilots and do one tour on an operational squadron. Consequently, he found himself sent to Canada to a small airfield called St Eugene, 50 miles west of Montreal, to be taught to fly.

As a Lieutenant of four years' standing, Goodhart was exalted in this company, all the rest on the course being newly-recruited Acting Leading Airmen and the instructors being Pilot Officers who had themselves only just learned to fly.

Half the day was devoted to flying and the other half to ground school and there was one day off every fortnight, so he was able to explain that he already knew all the ground school stuff and would happily take the exams when the time came but did not need to attend the instruction. That being so, he suggested that he should do his flying five days a week and 'get out of their hair' on Saturdays and Sundays.

With that agreement secured, Saturday mornings at 0430 hours, in temperatures of around minus 15C, would find him buckling on his skis and skiing the couple of miles to the station to catch the trans-Canada express.

On arrival at the station, which was completely un-manned at that time of day, the first thing to do – even before hugging the big pot-bellied stove still glowing gently in the waiting room – was to collect the red lantern put ready on the platform and carry it down to the west end so that it would be the first thing the train driver would see as he came round the corner.

Soon, as he stood there in that crisp, freezing silence, he would hear the train's ghostly hooter coming across the prairie and the enormous locomotive would come into view, all steam and noise with sparks flying from the brakes. He stood expectantly, skis on his shoulder, waiting to run as soon as the guard opened a door. Then he could climb, thankfully, into the warmth.

After changing trains at Montreal he would soon be at Mont Tremblant, where the skiing was excellent – as was the company of a pretty girl, with whom he was able to share more than the same standard of skiing.

Elementary Flying Training passed all too quickly, especially as its termination coincided with the end of the skiing season and so also meant the end of his friendship with that rather delightful girl, and he moved to Kingston, Ontario, for Service Flying Training, where compensation came in the form of the splendid sailing and swimming, which constituted the leisure activities. Meanwhile, at work he gained his FAA Wings in June 1944, flying Harvards.

After the grim days of the war, these were the very best of times – no more blackouts, light and good life all around, unlimited food of a variety which was no longer the stuff of dreams – but all good things come, sadly, to an end and his orders now were to grind himself through the laborious, tedious transport process to get, eventually, to some awful holding camp, there to wait interminably for the next transatlantic troopship.

However, if you're Nicholas Goodhart, orders are a challenge, not so much to be disobeyed as respectfully circumnavigated if you can, and so it was that he got home to the UK in just 24 hours by going, instead, to Montreal and hitching a lift in a Liberator. It was 31 days before the rest of 'his lot' were able to join up with him again. In August 1944 he moved to AFU Errol in Perthshire, flying Masters, then to NAFS Yeovilton in Somerset, flying Wildcats, before joining HMS *Smiter* for initial deck landing training in December 1944.

There was an unwelcome start to 1945 for Nicholas when he was hospitalised in RNH Sherborne for an internal operation but by the spring of that year he was back in action, being appointed to 896 Squadron (Hellcats) to join in the latter stages of the war with Japan.

Nicholas was later to describe what must have been a very dramatic stint, from May to September 1945, as a fighter pilot in the Burma campaign thus:

> 'I flew out as a passenger in an RAF Liberator. We didn't belong to one particular carrier but operated either from HMS *Emperor*, *Ameer* or *Empress* in the Indian Ocean for each operation. The task appeared to be mainly clearing up the remnants of the Japanese in Burma and Malaya. I had to ditch in the Malacca Straits due to engine failure but I was picked up OK by a destroyer, *Vigilant* and passed back to the carrier by jackstay.[5]'

This is yet another example of the way in which Nicholas so often employed understatement when describing events to which more dramatic language could be applied with absolute

---

[5] A *jackstay* is a rope to which a sail is fastened.

justification. 'Clearing up the remnants of the Japanese in Burma and Malaya' was, in fact, a highly dangerous operation with numerous British airmen losing their lives against some very fierce opposition, not least from Japanese *kamikaze* pilots. Goodhart was involved in intense flying and fighting, with several hundred sorties being flown by Hellcats.

Like many of his generation, Nicholas talked about his wartime experiences in a self-effacing, matter-of-fact style, peppered with humour, but when his war finally ended and he was selected for the Empire Test Pilots' Course, those experiences had been considerable and – although he would never hear of it – so had his courage.

4.   Goodhart the test pilot

AMONG THE MEN POSTED to join the test pilots' course at Cranfield in Bedfordshire in January 1946 were a few who stood out from the rest. They were the handful of Royal Navy officers who, simply because they were Royal Navy officers, were 'a bit different from the others'. And among those, standing out on his own even among that select group for being a bit different again, was one Lieutenant Commander Nicholas Goodhart.

There were several things about the smartly presented naval officer that made him different from his colleagues – the force of his personality and his sheer bloody-mindedness, among them. But, as far as his 32 course-mates were concerned, there was one rather more important thing that marked him out even more – his lack of flying experience. There was no avoiding the fact that, even though he had been able to build up his hours flying Seafires after being summoned back from the Far East the previous autumn, his experience was, at best, limited.

Most of the men on the course had clocked up more than 1,000 hours in the air, yet Goodhart had managed a mere 400. Even the next most inexperienced pilot – an RAF officer called David Ince, who had already proved his ability and bravery on active service from Normandy to the Baltic – had a rather more impressive 700 hours to his name. But 400? No wonder there were rumblings of discontent and the suspicion that someone in the Royal Navy had been pulling strings!

But if Nicholas's classmates were asking themselves what was so special about him to attract what they believed to be preferential treatment, they soon found out. While his lack of flying hours made him, in the language of the time, 'a sprog', they soon recognised that, despite his relative inexperience, he was a pilot to be reckoned with, and it was not long before he proved that he very much deserved to be on that course, despite the lack of hours in his log book.

And when it came to all other aspects of the group's training, he was not a sprog at all. From his desk at lectures – he always, typically, sat at the front, right under the nose of chief ground instructor Maclaren Humphries – he proved himself to be more than their equal. And not just because he was one of only two of them who knew how to use a slide rule. Nicholas was a man who knew his own mind, who knew he was right (even on the very rare occasions when he was wrong) and did not mind expressing his views, even to those who did not much want to hear them. He was not argumentative, exactly. Just very, very persuasive. And 'Humph' was remarkably tolerant.

'It wasn't much good debating with him because he was never willing to give an inch,' his old classmate and, later, friend and fellow glider pilot David Ince remembered. 'He could – and often did – argue you into the ground. He was always very confident, very assured and 90 per cent of the time he was absolutely right.'

It would be giving a false impression to suggest that Nicholas was unpopular on the course. He wasn't. But he wasn't popular either. 'People admired him rather than liked him,' Ince recalled. 'He was a bit nearer perfection than the rest. He was very single-minded about what he was going to do and that made him very difficult to get close to.'

In Ince's book *Brotherhood of the Skies* he admits that of all those on the course there was one – Goodhart – who 'eclipsed' the rest. 'You couldn't help admiring him,' Ince admitted. 'But it was hard on us lesser mortals. And in our youthful, less tolerant days, we were secretly pleased when Humph didn't let him get away with it.'

Partly because of his own personality and partly because, being one of the Naval minority on the course, he was therefore 'a bit different from the others', Nicholas always remained rather on the outside. So it's no surprise that not everything he did endeared him to either his class-mates or his instructors. On one occasion, for example, the course was given a Grunau Baby glider to evaluate as an aircraft – a task that required a detailed written appreciation following a modest test flight.

But Nicholas was less than interested in filling in the paper-work expected of him and very much more interested in seeing how far his prowess as a glider pilot would take him. While the other students were in the air for just a few minutes – time enough, they knew, to obtain all the information they required – he was gone for hours, unable to resist the temptation of the thermals which were just made for soaring. By the time he eventually landed he had been flying for far longer than all the others put together and was not even slightly shame-faced to admit that he had gained far less of the required technical information than anyone else.

To nobody's surprise (probably least of all to his own) Nicholas Goodhart graduated with distinction from the test pilots' course and was quickly appointed senior pilot of 700 Squadron at Yeovilton, teaching maintenance test flying to Navy pilots. This role – instructing pilots how to ensure that aircraft were fit for active service after they had been in for repair or servicing – could have been tailor-made for him, for it gave him the opportunity not just to fly an enormous variety of aircraft – Harvard, Barracuda, Firefly, Seafire, Master, Tiger Moth, Sea Otter and Firebrand – but to fly them always to the limit.

There seemed to be no stopping him in his quest to become one of the very best pilots in the Royal Navy. But if he needed a reminder of the dangers inherent in the job which was bringing him so much satisfaction, it came in the cruellest way on the afternoon of 15th October 1947.

Towards the end of a photo sortie, he was flying chase to the prototype Westland Wyvern with camera pundit Charles Brown in the rear seat. The new single-seat contraprop strike aircraft, specially designed to operate from carriers, was in the hands of Pete Garner, a squadron leader and old friend who by then was chief development test pilot at Westland. Pete liked the idea of Nicholas following behind to secure pictures of his revolutionary aircraft flying over such archetypal English landmarks as the Needles and Chesil Beach. It was a good day and the two men were in their element as they followed, one behind the other, looking for the best angles.

With the job done, they turned for home, heading back over the rolling countryside of southern England towards their base at Boscombe Down.

But it was soon clear that Garner was in trouble – and with something more than the usual handling issues that had dogged the Wyvern since its inception. Garner grappled with the controls but there was nothing even a pilot of his immense skill could do when the complex contraprop gearbox seized up. He dived steeply towards the ground in a desperate attempt to maintain speed and remain in control and it was obvious to Nicholas, watching from above, that he was trying to put the plane down in a field gently enough to avoid wrecking it altogether.

Even though he pulled out rather too late, bringing the Wyvern down in a heavy landing on its belly, it at first seemed that he had pulled off a miracle and the aircraft had suffered only minor damage. But it is almost certain that Garner had, in fact, been knocked out, or even killed, on impact and Goodhart could only watch helplessly from the sky as the Wyvern burst into flames.

Having to watch his friend die in such a fashion affected Goodhart deeply – something that those who had seen only the hard side of his character would have found surprising. But he was not the sort of man to allow his grief to get in the way of his duty – or his love of flying. And he knew that Garner would not have wanted it any other way. So when in the aftermath of Garner's death Westland asked the Navy if they could 'borrow' him to take over, temporarily, as test pilot for the Wyvern, he jumped at the chance.

He knew that after the crash the whole Wyvern project that had meant so much to Garner was in doubt – not least because Westland were having trouble finding any other test pilots for a plane that was fast developing a reputation as very dangerous (in fact it went on to claim several more lives, not just Garner's). So if nothing else, he reasoned, his accepting the job was a way of ensuring that the project to which his friend had devoted so much time, energy and skill would not die with him.

Having effectively 'rescued' the Wyvern project, Nicholas returned to the Navy and, for the next three years, advanced his career by further developing his skills flying more than 100 different types of aircraft as a test pilot. In May 1948 he moved to Donibristle Naval Aircraft Repair Yard as maintenance test pilot, flying anything from Tiger Moths and Seafires to Harvards and Fireflies but, within a few weeks, had moved again –

to Boscombe Down's Intensive Flying Development Flight, where he flew Sea Hornets, Vampires and Meteors, before adding Sturgeons, Ertcoupes and Mamba Balliols to his list after joining Boscombe's C Squadron.

Of this time, writing in 2007, he drew a comparison between the attitudes of pilots flying in the immediate postwar years and 'today'.

'I was in 'C' Squadron at Boscombe Down in 1949, where our job was to put the many new naval aircraft emerging from the manufacturers through their paces in order to accept them (or not) as meeting the RN requirement. As an indication of the way things were, I see from my log book that in March 1950 I flew 34 sorties in 20 days on nine totally different types of aircraft. Five were piston-engined, two were pure jets and two were prop-jets.

'Small wonder that in those days flying a new type was simply a question of finding somebody who had already flown it and getting them to show you round the cockpit and mention any peculiar habits it had. Later, often much later, one picked up details of the systems and emergency procedures.

'Compare that with today when it probably takes a month of instruction before you even see a real aircraft.

'One morning I had a Sturgeon to take down to Lee-on-Solent. The weather was foul with a solid cloud base at about 1000ft and visibility of about a mile, however one new the area pretty well so I could get along alright at about 800ft. In a short while I was bumbling along over Southampton and thought I would explore the one engine out capability of the aircraft so I shut down the port engine and feathered the propeller. This was entirely satisfactory with a bit more throttle on the starboard engine and a bit of rudder to counteract the offset thrust.

'Of course, if one had to land with one engine out one would expect to use some flap. So I put the flaps down and found a very different picture. With full throttle on the live engine we could not maintain altitude. So I hastily selected flaps up. Nothing happened. There was no hydraulic power. This was getting serious. The rooftops were getting much too close. We needed the port engine and quickly. Unfeathering and a windmill start seemed to take an age (a few seconds actually) and luckily the engine caught at once and, what is more, the flaps started to come up. Big sigh of relief.

'I later found out that there was only one hydraulic pump which was on the port engine. This was done as a weight saving measure. As you can guess I did not support it.'

Through it all, most people who met Nicholas would have used such words as 'determined', 'single-minded' or 'ambitious' to describe him. His old friend David Ince was one of the few who got to know him well enough to detect the more caring side to his nature but it was many years before that more compassionate dimension of his complex personality truly showed itself.

Indeed, it may only have been in 2009, by which time he was 89 years old, that some of his former colleagues saw the 'new'– or perhaps the real – Nicholas Goodhart. The occasion was a reunion of test pilots at Popham airfield in Hampshire, which he and Ince attended together. Ince recalls that Nicholas briefly swapped yarns and memories with some of those he recognised and who, like him, were still hale and hearty, but noticeably cut his conversations with them short so he could spend more time talking to those who to whom the years had been less kind.

One such was Alan Bristow, who after the war had gone on to make his name building and operating helicopters but was now in a wheelchair after suffering a stroke. Another was Dickie Martin, who in the war had become famous by escaping from a prison camp in Luxembourg before making his way home to re-join his squadron for the Battle of France.

Goodhart spent a lot of time talking to them both – even though it meant ignoring some of the others whom he knew better and who had once been closer to him. When Ince asked him why he had spent so much time with them at the expense of men with whom he had more in common, Nicholas explained that those who were fit and healthy could manage to look after themselves and enjoy the day without any assistance from him, while those like Bristow and Martin needed special help if they were going to get the most from the occasion.

Even Ince, one of the few who had glimpsed the more considerate side of Nicholas's nature, was taken aback. 'He said he was looking after the lame ducks, which I found quite surprising at the time,' he said later. 'It was another side of the man, which not even those of us who counted ourselves as his friends saw very often.'

5.   Goodhart's Court Martial

EARLY NAVAL TRAINING had established in the mind of Nicholas Goodhart that courts martial were the ultimate, absolute naval penalty used only in the event of appalling wrongdoing and hardly relevant to the ordinary and reasonably respectable naval officer – a breed of which he considered himself an example.

So it came as a shock, to say the least, when, completely out of the blue, he was commanded by Their Lordships of the Admiralty to present himself on board HMS *Victory* on Monday 12th April 1949 to be court martialled on a charge which amounted to 'hazarding one of His Majesty's aircraft'. This was the 'air' version of the more familiar charge preferred against Captains of HM ships and he was astounded.

The only saving grace to cushion the blow was that at least it was not one of those 'unmentionable' crimes which were often the subject of courts martial and heaped on the hapless defendant the additional ignominy of notoriety through the columns of the *News Of The World*.

In 1949 Goodhart was at the height of his flying career.

He was serving as a test pilot in the Naval Squadron at Boscombe Down, where they were clearing a host of new post war naval aircraft designs for introduction (or not, as the case might be) into service use. Particularly in the latter half of the war, all the UK aircraft firms had been fully engaged in designing and building aircraft for the RAF, leaving the Navy to depend on Lend/Lease from the United States.

Not surprisingly, therefore, the industry responded with enthusiasm to a post-war rash of new specifications issued for naval aircraft and Boscombe was consequently very busy. For example, Goodhart's log book shows 46 flying hours in the month of May on 13 entirely separate types of aircraft of which two were jets, two were prop jets and the rest were piston-engined.

The incident that led to his court martial had occurred in February when he had been doing a test on a Vampire. He was required to fly along the runway as low and as slow as he reasonably could while observers timed him over a marked distance to compute his airspeed.

At the same time, he had to read a special air speed indicator mounted externally on the skin of the aircraft just in front of the windscreen. The aim was to find out the errors of the air speed measuring system at deck landing speeds.

The test was intended to be conducted wheels-down but, in concentrating on the external air speed indicator, he failed to put the wheels down. Had he just glanced down in the cockpit, as he would have done in order to read the normal ASI, he would have been alerted by a blaze of red lights. In any case, he had not been intending to land – but at the slow speed he was attempting to maintain the aircraft was in a steep nose-up attitude and, because he had not allowed sufficiently for the tailboom bumpers[6] being well below the nose, they just touched the runway.

---

[6] The de Havilland company produced a small number of early jet aircraft designs with tricycle undercarriages – a nosewheel with the main wheels behind the centre of gravity – and twin tail booms to carry the empennage. Flown at minimum speed it was possible to get the booms lower than the

In this situation, he no longer had vertical control of the aircraft which then descended gently onto its belly on the runway and slid to a stop – with a somewhat 'scraped' lower engine cowling.

Quite a kerfuffle ensued, with first a fire crew then a crane crew rushing out to the runway but the aircraft was quickly removed and everything soon returned to normal. To cool-headed pilot Goodhart, this had all been in a day's work. He knew that he had made a stupid mistake but events of this nature were not uncommon and he expected little more than a red endorsement in his log book, accompanied by some inevitable loss of face at having made such an error.

Nothing was said at the time, nothing happened and the incident appeared to have been forgotten, seemingly lost in the huge pressure of work being loaded on to the Naval Test Squadron at the time – all of which served to make Their Lordships' letter informing him that he was to be court martialled even more shocking.

The week before his court martial, Goodhart was instructed to go to Lee-on-Solent on the Friday, in order to be available at 0900 hours on the jetty beside HMS *Victory* on the Monday. As soon as he had completed Friday's flying, he jumped into his Auster and, half an hour later, was at Lee-on-Solent, where he was met by a nervous young Lieutenant to whom, apparently, had fallen the task of ensuring that he did not fail to turn up for his court martial.

The pair hit an immediate difficulty. So far as Goodhart was concerned, he had no duties to perform over the weekend so he

---

wheels. They were, therefore, fitted with rubber bumpers to avoid any damage to the structure when slow flying near the ground. Similar problems arose with other aircraft until pilots, trained on what are now known as 'tail-draggers' became more familiar with the new tricycle designs.

told his young custodian that he would go off on weekend leave on the Saturday morning and return on Sunday evening. This deeply concerned the Lieutenant, who clearly considered it his duty to keep Goodhart under observation until the court martial.

Goodhart was having none of that and there was much panic and reference to higher authority before it was established that he was not under arrest and there was therefore no valid reason why he shouldn't go off on leave. He assured the Lieutenant that he would most certainly return, as promised, on Sunday evening but the young man spent 24 hours chewing his nails to the quick before Goodhart touched down on the airfield at the agreed time and put him out of his misery.

At 0900 hours the dockyard echoed to a huge *boom!* as the court martial gun was fired aboard HMS *Victory*. Immediately, the members of the court trooped up the gangway and into Nelson's dining room.

As soon as they were ready, Goodhart was marched on board, with the fretful young Lieutenant behind him, carrying a bared sword at the ready. Goodhart supposed that this was in preparation to bury it in his ribs if he tried to run away but the young man needn't have worried because by this time the defendant was fully adjusted to the whole event and had started to rather look forward to it all.

Once in the court, the first thing required of Goodhart was to lay his own sword on the table in front of the president of the court martial. There was no dock as such, so he had to stand back from the table with the young Lieutenant, sword still bared, standing behind him.

While the initial proceedings were taking place, he had the opportunity to observe the members of the court. They were verging on the geriatric – i.e. at least 20 years older than him –

and clearly knew nothing whatsoever about flying. Then he spotted that there was one who had wings on his arm. 'Ah, an ally,' he thought – until it occurred to him that these wings were of a type which had been discontinued in 1937.

'Oh dear,' Goodhart muttered to himself, 'he'll think that aeroplanes have two wings, a fixed undercarriage and a rumbling old piston engine enabling them to do 100 knots or so and that only downhill with a following wind.'

Typically, Goodhart had chosen to conduct his own defence, which gave him the advantage of having the last say. He had also ensured that a reporter from the *Portsmouth Evening News* was present because he had some things to say which Their Lordships would probably prefer not to be widely publicised.

About a quarter of an hour after the start of proceedings, the young Lieutenant was beginning to realise that standing with a bared sword at the ready was remarkably wearing on the arm. Then he noticed that the point of the sword was just under a deep crack in the overhead timber.

Without further ado and with much relief he eased the point into the crack until it jammed and he was able to suspend his arm comfortably. Shortly afterwards, the president announced suddenly: 'Gentlemen, you may be seated.' As Goodhart sat down, he saw with great amusement that this instruction had left an exceedingly embarrassed young Lieutenant trying desperately to extricate his sword from the beam into which it had chosen to jam so solidly.

The main witness for the prosecution was the Engineer Officer at Boscombe Down, a Wing Commander, who gave evidence that he had personally climbed into the cockpit as soon as the crane had lifted the aircraft from the ground, had selected the undercarriage down and had then, with the aid of the manual hydraulic pump, been able to pump the undercarriage down until it locked. Ergo, the undercarriage mechanism was in good working order.

Goodhart observed, with considerable further amusement, that all of this evidence was clearly a total mystery to the court:

'Why were the wheels not under the aeroplane, anyway?'

'Hydraulics? What on earth have they got to do with it?'

'What happened to the propeller?'

However, the Wing Commander struggled manfully on until eventually satisfied that he had proved beyond doubt that the aircraft was serviceable and hence that the accident had been caused by pilot error.

Then it was Goodhart's turn.

He had found in his pilot's notes booklet for the Vampire a paragraph which stated unequivocally that in the event of the engine-driven hydraulic pump not working, there was enough reserve in the hydraulic accumulator to put both the flaps and the undercarriage down once. He called the Wing Commander back to explain to the court why, when he selected 'undercarriage down', the hydraulic accumulator had not done its duty and he had had to resort to the hand pump.

This appeared to throw the witness into some confusion and he launched into a rambling explanation, which achieved only further bafflement of the court. Finally, the president admitted that he did not understand:

'Why did the wheels not come down when you selected 'down'?'

The Wing Commander had had enough and replied, rather pathetically, 'I don't know.'

Sensing that this had completely destroyed the prosecution's case, Goodhart moved quickly on to what he thought was the court's home ground. He told them:

'Remember that I was driving a machine in three dimensions which had a minimum speed of three times the maximum of the ships with which you are familiar. I had no bevy of signalmen to handle communications, no team of engineers to control the engine, no quartermaster to steer, no navigator to determine the course, no lookouts to look for other aircraft. It all fell to me and, in addition, I was conducting this special test. Small wonder, therefore, that I forgot to put the wheels down and, due to having the external ASI, did not see the red lights in the cockpit.'

Whoops! The collective sigh of relief from the court was almost audible as they realised all their difficulties had evaporated. Goodhart had admitted that he had made a mistake and that the aircraft had undoubtedly been hazarded. They were not interested in his mitigating plea of an extraordinarily heavy workload.

Without further ado, he and his faithful young shadow were sent out while the court considered its verdict.

After a disturbingly short interval they were summoned back into court. The verdict was immediately obvious. In time honoured tradition Goodhart's sword now lay on the table with its point towards him. The president announced that he had been found guilty as charged and that he was adjudged to be reprimanded.

It was Goodhart's understanding that this meant that he would, in due course, receive Their Lordships' displeasure on vellum. Compensation, he reckoned, because he could think of nothing more appropriate to hang on the wall of the smallest room in his house.

'Sadly,' he recalled years later, 'this was not to be.'

For when he rang the Naval Secretary's office a few weeks after his trial, he learned that Their Lordships had decided to quash the conviction and annul the sentence.

Nicholas Goodhart with Bill Ivans, the American champion who lent him the glider in which he set the 37,050ft altitude record in 1955. The glider in which Bill is sitting is the Schweizer SGS 1-23 – the very machine that made Nicholas a world-beater.

Nicholas (second from right) with Stan Smith (second from left) at Idlewild (now JFK) Airport on 7th July 1953. The American – shown here with fellow glider pilot Bernie Carris (centre) and three officials from National Airlines – had just won a competition as first pilot to land during the National Soaring Contest at an airport served by the airline.

Left to right: Bob Smith, Kemp Trager, Nicholas Goodhart at Harris Hill airfield near Elmira, New York State in the mid-1950s.

Left to right: Paul Schweizer, Nicholas Goodhart, Bernard (Barney) Wiggin and Hugh Whitney at Camphill airfield, home of the Derby and Lancs Gliding Club during the 1954 World Gliding Championships. Paul and Nicholas were both leading international glider pilots at the time; Barney was the US team manager and meteorologist; Hugh was Paul's crew chief.

Nicholas and David Ince take to the skies above Lasham in Hampshire in the spring of 1958. In this picture, taken by Charles Brown, Nicholas is nearest the camera in the second prototype Eon 419, which he was to fly in the 1960 World Championships at Butsweilerhof near Cologne in 1960. David is flying the EoN 415 in which he was to win the National Aerobatic Championships in September 1958.

An 'officer of undoubted intelligence and ability'
promoted to Rear Admiral in 1972.

Nicholas lands his private Auster on the deck of HMS *Bulwark* in 1956.
'He was probably just going there for lunch,' says Molly.

Molly learned to fly gliders too – winning the genuine respect of men
in what was then a male-dominated environment.

Nicholas, when a cadet at Dartmouth – he found it
'a steep learning curve, rich in fascination and interest'.

February 1962 – now a Captain.

Molly – Nicholas's 'first and only real love'.

Nicholas and Molly – 'a marriage that was to endure happily for nearly 40 years'.

Nicholas showing a model of his Sigma glider to the Duke of Edinburgh in 1969.
Prince Philip was one of the project's most enthusiastic supporters.

Nicholas Goodhart – for 20 years one of the best glider pilots in the world.

Nicholas and his old friend David Ince at a reunion
of test pilots at Popham airfield in Hampshire.

Nicholas in the robes of the Master of the City Guild of Grocers.

Nicholas stands in for Father Christmas for the
benefit of his neighbours' grandchildren in Devon.

Nicholas in the tranquil surroundings of Lindridge – the
lovely home that meant so much to him.

Skiing – just another of the many activities at which Nicholas excelled.

Nicholas shows his interest in all things technical
as a Rear Admiral in the Ministry of Defence.

6.   Goodhart the glider pilot

ON THE VERY DAY that the war in Europe ended – VE Day, 8th May 1945 – Lieutenant Commander John Sproule, based in Lee-on-Solent but apparently with more time on his hands than he needed to do the little work required of him, began to put into action a plan he had been nursing for some time.

He was desperately keen to re-start the flourishing gliding career that Hitler and his troops had brought to a temporary halt five years before, so had been giving a lot of thought to how best it could be done. And he soon realised that the old enemy could be the key . . .

Under the Treaty of Versailles, signed at the end of the First World War, the Germans had been ordered to destroy all their fighting aircraft and, to prevent them rebuilding their military capability, had been forbidden to develop any sort of military air force.[7] However, there was nothing in the treaty that pre-vented them from flying gliders, so they took up the sport in huge numbers – and with great success.

The German authorities saw gliding as a means of instilling in a large number of young men (and some young women) the sort of flying skills which – who knew? – might one day come in useful again. So with the flair and efficiency typical of their

---

[7] In fact, German pilots went on being trained in secret, either masquerading as rookie airline pilots for Lufthansa or training as combat pilots with the help of the Russians at a clandestine airbase at Lipetsk, 300 or so miles south of Moscow.

race, they developed a whole range of new gliders on which they could hone their skills. And, since those gliders were considerably more advanced than anything that could be found anywhere else, in the years between the wars Germany had some of the best glider pilots in the world, flying some of the best gliders ever invented.

To Sproule, starved of gliding since 1939, the temptation of all those fine German gliders was too much to resist, so he resolved that he would contrive to get his hands on some of them as a kind of reparation. He realised that going through approved channels was almost certain to fail, so he wrote himself some orders and – along with three sailors, a low loader and a 'Tilly' (a small van that could carry four people and still have room for plenty of baggage) – he set off for Dover.

Catching a ferry turned out to be no problem and nor – thanks to help from some British soldiers, who provided the bizarre little group with food, petrol and somewhere to stop for the night – did getting to Germany. Once across the border, Sproule and his men, obeying the orders he had written for himself, headed straight for a gliding site that he had visited before the war. He found the site under the control of the British Army, but they were entirely happy with what he was doing, so he and his men – and four German gliders – were back at Lee-on-Solent within a week.

On his return Sproule found that senior officers in the Royal Navy had come to realise the importance of what they called 'air-mindedness' among their men, so they allowed him to use the four gliders commandeered from Germany to form the Royal Naval Gliding Flight. It was a decision which was to have a profound effect on the life of Nicholas Goodhart when, after 'thumbing a lift' in an RAF freight aircraft, he returned to Britain from the Far East three months later.

Once back in the UK, Nicholas discovered he had been selected for the Empire Test Pilots' course at Boscombe Down in Wiltshire, which by good fortune happened to be within easy reach of Lee-on-Solent and, more importantly, within easy reach of John Sproule and his small fleet of gliders.

For Nicholas and his brother Tony – both 'impecunious young naval officers,' as he put it – this was a heaven-sent opportunity to rekindle their passion for gliding and catch up on some of the flying experience they had missed by going to war. They were able to improve their still relatively basic skills by circuit after circuit around (and a little soaring above) the Lee-on-Solent airfield – sometimes in the company of a group of cadets from Dartmouth, who were encouraged to give up some of their summer leave to gain their first experience of gliding.

Nicholas's comprehensive flying log books show that his first post-war flight was on 26th February 1946, when he managed seven minutes free flight in a requisitioned Grunau Baby – a German glider he had never flown before – after a ten-minute tow behind one of the Navy's Tiger Moths.

He took every opportunity he could find to get into the air, although few of his flights lasted more than just a few minutes and – thanks in part to the high quality of the German gliders (two of them were high-performance single-seaters) and the frequency at which they were able to fly – the Goodhart brothers were able to make rapid progress.

Nicholas's log book shows that it was not until 20th April 1947 that he managed a soaring flight worthy of the name – when he stayed airborne for 48 minutes by cashing in on rising air above Cock Hill, a small ridge of higher land near a gliding club at Westonzoyland, a village in the area of Somerset flatland known as The Levels.

Westonzoyland had had an airfield for many years and during the war had been used for glider and parachute training by the US Air Force in their preparations for D-Day, so the sight of Nicholas taking off from there and circling above their heads in his open-cockpit Kirby Kadet (an aircraft designed by his old friend John Sproule when he worked for Slingsby Sailplanes) should have been of no special note to the locals. But it was a sensation!

Hundreds of people – perhaps seeing Nicholas's old-fashioned plywood machine as a welcome sign that life was at last beginning to return to normal after the war years – turned out to watch, heads cocked backwards as they stared into the sky until, when all sign of lift disappeared from beneath his wings, he had no option but to head for home. Even the local paper was excited enough to record the event, under the headline 'Why they stopped!'.

'Motor coach parties and motorists were among the several hundreds of people who stopped on the Bridgwater-Glastonbury road on Sunday to witness the first soaring flight arranged by the local gliding club,' it reported. 'Pilot of the machine was Lieut. N Goodhart RN, who only recently joined the club. He kept the machine aloft for just under an hour.'

If Nicholas was looking for something more exciting in his gliding career than simply flying around the sky for the fun of it (and he was!) he found it a few months later, when John Sproule invited him to co-pilot one of the two-seater Kranichs in the National Gliding Competitions at RNAS Bramcote near Nuneaton.

Nicholas found the extra dimension of competitive gliding fitted perfectly with his personality. Not for nothing did his old wartime comrade David Ince later describe him thus:

'Forceful, brilliant and ambitious, with a single-mindedness which would take him to the top unless he upset too many people on the way. Nicholas Goodhart was one of those infuriating individuals who knew he was right and, on the rare occasions when he was wrong, could still drive his opponents into the ground with the force of his arguments and his personality.'

Such a character needed an outlet for his competitive spirit – and he found it in the challenge of pitting his wits and his blossoming skills against the country's top glider pilots.

Even though he and Sproule managed only one significant flight (nearly two hours) during the championships, it was at Bramcote that his love of competition flying was inspired. This, he decided, was the real thing! Not only was he rubbing shoulders and talking to the gliding 'gods' he had hitherto only worshipped from afar, he was being given the opportunity to compare his talents with theirs.

He was not so arrogant as to believe that he could yet compete with men such as these. Philip Wills was one of the real pioneers of British gliding, the holder of several records and a long-time member of the British team. Geoffrey Stephenson was another pioneer who had been the first Briton to fly a glider across the English Channel. And Kit Nicholson was the British champion and another record holder who was to die on a mist-shrouded mountain top during the 1948 World Gliding Championship in Switzerland.

No, Nicholas Goodhart knew he could not yet compete with them. But he was still young. And there was time...

In early 1949 Nicholas gave his gliding career a boost by purchasing a powered aircraft and building a little airfield for it at his parents' home at Inkpen. Nicholas was working at that time as technical secretary to the admiral responsible for procuring the naval aircraft for the Fleet Air Arm, a job which involved little more than organising his boss's official visits to aircraft manufacturers and accompanying him there to support him.

The second-hand Auster he bought for £625 would come in useful, he decided, in getting him around the country – especially as the aircraft companies he was visiting would always refuel it for him for free and the admiralty would pay him the equivalent car mileage allowance for the much longer journey he would otherwise have had to take by road.

But, more than that, the little Auster would enable him and his brother to travel quickly and efficiently to the various gliding sites – both in Britain and in mainland Europe – they wanted to visit to build up their expertise. And if it would enable them also to hop across the English Channel for weekends in France, so much the better!

Flying to France in those days was an adventure (and Nicholas enjoyed adventures). There was none of the rationing there that there was in post-war England and the mood in France was decidedly more upbeat, so the *entente* was always extremely *cordiale* after the two flying brothers landed their Auster in whichever foreign field they chose.

The dead hand of officialdom had yet to destroy the excitement of puttering across the Channel in your own plane. No formalities had to be observed, and no permission requested, all Nicholas had to do was throw a dinghy in the back of his plane and set course for the extravagant welcome he knew would be in store wherever and whenever he landed.

'Wherever we went,' he recalled later, 'we were greeted with acclaim. That inevitably meant a *vin d'honneur* or two – and things usually went downhill from there.'

The brothers visited gliding sites in France, Switzerland and Spain – Nicholas's logbook is full of such evocative names as Cannes, Zurich and Huesca – and took every opportunity to understand and master the differing and unfamiliar soaring conditions abroad. It was a vital part of the learning curve. Both were familiar with the principles and practice of wave and thermal flying but in the South of France and over the Alps conditions were considerably different from – or at least more extreme than – either of them had experienced before in England.

Both Nicholas and Tony made rapid progress and, in April 1950 at Challes-les-Eaux in France, Nicholas flew high and long enough to secure those two essential components towards his 'Silver C' badge, the first major qualification the serious glider pilot sets his sights upon.

By then he was beginning to be good enough to pit his skills against some of the top names in the sport, so he started entering the competitions which the British Gliding Association – after a three-year hiatus following what had become known as 'The Bramcote Affair'– had started to organise once again. The BGA had learned its lesson from the 1947 National Gliding Competitions at RNAS Bramcote, at which Nicholas had got his first taste of competitive flying while co-piloting with John Sproule. That event, much though Nicholas had enjoyed it, had been organised on far too grand a scale and was a financial disaster.

The BGA set up its next two Nationals at Camphill in the Peak District of Derbyshire. The one in 1949 was hit by poor weather but 1950 was a considerable success. It was a considerable success for Nicholas too. With his self-assured nature, he was comfortably at home among the country's top pilots, even though the glider he was flying – the Navy's Mu 13 – makes a surprising comparison with those of his fellow competitors. The Mu 13 was a magnificent lightweight soaring machine. It would stay up in the weakest of lift when everything else was falling out of the sky. Yet it totally lacked penetration – an ability to fly at the flattest possible gliding angle at the highest possible speed. The few instruments it had were, in Nicholas's judgement, 'pretty useless'.

Yet in five competitive flights he won two prizes for the biggest gain of height of the day and, with one 2½ hour flight from Camphill to Boston in Lincolnshire, won equal top marks with Philip Wills, the doyen of glider pilots at the time, who was flying a high-performance German Weihe glider.

Nicholas – who had never managed a successful cross-country flight before – claimed no great merit for this latter feat. It was, he said, 'a case of good luck rather than good judgement' that enabled him to fly a rather primitive glider as well as Wills had flown his top-of-the-range one. But, good luck or not, the 85 mile flight to the east coast had not just completed the missing cross-country component of his Silver C, it had brought him, in emphatic style, to the notice of the top echelon of British glider pilots. And it set him on a course of competition flying that was to play a key part of his life for the next twenty years.

Nicholas was not conscious of having any particular long-term ambition in gliding. He was just enjoying the challenge of getting the best out of himself and his glider at each succeeding competition. The fun was in the competition, not the gliding. He did not even find the flying particularly enjoyable (many of the flights ended with him nursing a splitting headache), although there were, he admitted later, some 'wonderful times'.

Coming out of a cumulonimbus thundercloud at 20,000ft, with the whole world seemingly spread out like a map below and the unbelievable brilliance of the great white wall of cloud behind, was something he always found 'a transcendental moment', although too often he had little time to enjoy it. There was always too much to do.

'Where are we?' 'What speed should I fly now there is at least 300lb of ice on the wings?' 'Should I switch off the artificial horizon device to conserve the battery?' 'Is the oxygen OK?' and, most important of all, 'What is the sky like ahead and where is the next lift to come from?' Perhaps even (but only for a moment), 'By golly, I'm very cold, sopping wet, miserable and hungry...'

Nicholas's gliding career was going from strength to strength, though often, typically, it was in a rather unorthodox manner. In May 1951, for example, he travelled to Pont Saint Vincent, a village near Nancy in eastern France, which boasted its own small hilltop airfield, famous for being surrounded by small stone slabs, each recording the name of a glider pilot who had been killed there. Into this unlikely setting stepped Nicholas Goodhart who, having no glider of his own there, borrowed one and, having no map, calmly unwrapped his sandwiches, drew a few basic details onto the greaseproof paper they were contained in, before setting off on a near 200-mile goal flight, with which he secured the distance component of his Gold C badge and his first Diamond C leg.

As if anyone needed reminding that he was a glider pilot of enormous potential, he underlined the fact a couple of months later by winning the Club entered competition for older gliders at the British Nationals, which were again being held at Camphill. His brother came second. On 23rd April 1952 – less than two years after completing his Silver C badge – he completed his Gold C, an altogether more notable achievement. This required him to fly a distance of 300 kilometres, gain 3,000 metres in height and stay airborne for at least five hours (though not necessarily all in the same flight). He did it with a climb to a height of 13,300ft with a bit of help from a 'cu-nim' (*cumulonimbus* cloud) over Odiham in Hampshire.

Such feats – and such rapid progress – were not going unnoticed by those at the very top of the sport and it was not long before he gained his first experience of international competition when he was asked to crew for Philip Wills at the 1952 World Championships in Spain.

It was no doubt a blow to British gliding when, at the end of 1952, the Navy promoted him to Commander and despatched him across the Atlantic on RMS *Queen Elizabeth* to take up a post as Staff Air Engineer Officer and Staff Pilot with the British Joint Services Mission in Washington DC. But for Nicholas it was just another challenge – in both his naval and his gliding careers.

He was almost immediately adopted by the American gliding fraternity – who thought nothing of lending him their aircraft, giving him whatever other help he needed and generally treating him as one of their own – and in July 1953 he achieved the remarkable distinction of coming fifth in the US National Soaring Championships in Elmira, New York State, after his American friends lent him one of their old wartime training gliders.

The end of 1954 marked the start of an extraordinary period in Nicholas's gliding career. His time in the USA had already paid off by his being invited to crew for the American No 1 pilot Paul MacCready in that year's World Championships at Camphill in England, but by Christmas his own flying was taking on a new dimension.

On 9th January 1955, flying Bill Ivans' Schweizer 1-23, he took a tow to 10,500ft above Bishop, California and went on to climb another 20,000ft, unaided by anything other than rising air and his own skill. That was more than enough to qualify for the height component of his Diamond C badge, which requires only that a pilot manages to gain 5,000 metres (16,400ft).

On May 12 he achieved the British Absolute Altitude Record in the feat with which we began this account of his life and, on August 19, a borrowed Weihe carried him 318 miles across Texas, from Dallas to Amarillo, in a flight lasting more than 7½ hours. It was only the 100th time anyone in the world had flown more than 500km in a glider and, more importantly, it wrote him into the record books as the first British person to complete all three components for the Diamond 'C' badge.

And, on top of it all, he scored more points than anyone else in the 22nd US National Soaring Championships, once again staged at Elmira, New York State! In an extraordinary nine days flying, he was airborne for more than 85 hours, covering well over 920 miles – but not even that was enough for him to be anointed American Champion. Being British he was not allowed to win the American trophy, so instead was hailed as 'above the champion'. His American friends, realising the injustice of the situation, clubbed together and presented him with his own special trophy – an award which he treasured nearly as much as he would have if he had been given the real thing.

His success was marked by an article in the *Washington Post*, which, under the headline 'Sail Plane Pilot Back At Embassy Job Here', reported:

> 'Commander HCN Goodhart – a man likely to be found hugging the edge of a cumulus cloud with only the gossamer wings of a sail plane between him and the ground – returned to his desk at the British Embassy yesterday.
>
> 'The past two weeks he's been soaring over the hills and lakes around Elmira, N.Y., competing in the 22nd annual soaring championships there. He beat the best sail plane pilots in

America but was declared ineligible for the title because he isn't a United States citizen.

'Longest hop was from Elmira to Wilmington, Del – nearly 200 miles – which Goodhart did in 5 hours 47 minutes. 'An indescribable pleasure,' is the way the 35-year-old Royal Navy officer defines soaring. 'Two months ago I went up to 37,000 feet over the Sierra Nevadas in California. It was absolutely delightful. The scenery was superb; the silence complete.'

'A typical sail plane weighs 350 pounds, is 18 feet long with a 45 foot wing span. It is made of wood or aluminium and costs about 3,500 dollars. The usual method of taking off is to get a tow from a power plane or a truck. The trick to staying aloft is to find an updraft and gain altitude by circling upward around its center. When the updraft has carried the plane as high as possible the pilot glides towards his destination. Meanwhile, he seeks another updraft because if he doesn't find one there is nothing to do but come down.

'Best updrafts are found under newly forming cumulus clouds. 'I spend hours watching the life cycles of cumulus clouds,' Goodhart reports. 'They only last half an hour, you know, before they disappear. The most exciting part of soaring is circling your way up in a thermal. When you enter you feel a slight turbulence, a bubbling sensation. The thing is alive. It effervesces. The plane gives an upward heave and you bank sharply 'til you find the center. That's where the art and skill come in – knowing how to keep in the center of the updraft and how fast to climb without stalling.'

'Goodhart, who enjoys nothing more than poking a sail plane into a small thunderstorm, was a Royal Navy cadet at 13. He has 22 years of military service behind him, which includes duty on cruisers and carriers during World War Two and four years as a test pilot. 'Wonderful work, test piloting,' says Goodhart. 'Laziest work in the world.'

'With all the awards he has won, the only achievement left for him is to earn a Gold C with three diamonds for a flight of 312 miles. Fifteen Americans hold this award but no Englishman has won it yet. As Goodhart points out: 'You can't fly 312 miles in Great Britain without going over the edge. Besides, Americans have the advantage of Texas updrafts which, like everything else in that state, are bigger and better than anywhere else in the world.'

Not all of Nicholas's gliding in America was quite so successful. He was the first to admit that, while it was his competitive streak that enabled him to compete so well with the world's top pilots, it was also that which sometimes led him into trouble.

On one flight, for example, he spotted a nice flat-bottomed cloud building up a couple of miles away. It was precisely what he was looking for – a sign of the rising air that could take him on yet another memorable flight. The only possible problem, he noticed, was a patch of *mammatus* cloud on the way, and that, as he knew very well, was a sure sign of sinking, not rising air. He could easily have doglegged around it to reach the cu-nim on the other side, but he was flying at 3,500ft and that, he reckoned, was high enough. The cloud was no more than half a mile wide and it would take only a few seconds to pass across it, so he decided to make a dash through it.

He put the glider's nose down to increase his speed and headed towards it. He hit the sinking air just as he knew he would, but was still flying fast enough and high enough to safely reach the other side. Then, as he put it later, 'the bottom fell out of the sky'. The glider was sinking rapidly – the landscape below him visibly expanding – and he could do nothing about it. The needles of the variometers, which at better moments would have been indicating his rate of climb, were stuck on their backstops, telling him he was losing height so fast they could not even register it.

For one less skilled than Nicholas it could have been fatal. Not many glider pilots have the ability to recover from such a dramatic and sudden loss of height but, in less than a minute, he had managed to make an emergency landing in an accommodating field which, by pure good fortune, just happened to be beneath him when he at last managed to regain control of the glider.

It was an experience from which he should have learned the lesson: *never take a risk by pushing yourself too far.* He *should* have learned it but, of course, he didn't. And his gliding career would have been far less successful if he had!

After such a successful spell in America, Nicholas had mixed feelings about coming back to England. He had enjoyed the challenge of working there and enjoyed even more the company of so many good friends who had helped him achieve such remarkable feats as a glider pilot.

His return was marked by one piece of unexpected good news. His prowess as a glider pilot – proved so often, so consistently and so dramatically over the previous five years or so – was at last being recognised. The British Gliding Association had selected him for the team to represent his country in the Sixth World Championships – to be held at Saint Yan, near Lyon in France the following June.

He was not particularly pleased to find that he was to fly in the two-seater class, because his personality was more suited to flying solo than as part of a team. But he was in the team and wasn't going to complain – especially when he discovered who had been chosen to be his co-pilot team-mate.

Frank Foster was a British European Airways airline pilot who, in the 11 years he had been flying gliders, had become something of a pioneer in cross-country missions. He was a charming and equable man yet, once in a glider's cockpit, a bit of a daredevil. His attitude was that if there were thermals over an airfield there would be thermals further away, so he should go and find them – a strategy that frequently saw him flying just a little bit further than some people might have considered strictly sensible.

In that respect Frank was a perfect partner for Nicholas, who, admitting that he too sometimes had a touch of recklessness about him, confessed years later: 'I was particularly bad at pushing on when the probabilities were all against me.'

The glider provided for Nicholas and Frank's assault on the World Championships in June 1956 was a Slingsby Eagle T42B – not a glider renowned for its high performance – and the only consolation was that the opposition were not much better.

However Nicholas revelled in the competitive nature of the World Championships. This was the most impressive array of top glider pilots ever assembled, with a record 25 countries being represented. The unpredictable weather conditions were a real challenge to even the most experienced pilots, with every soaring skill taxed to the limit – and, very often, far beyond. Even a pilot as accomplished as Bill Ivans, Nicholas's old American friend who had lent him his Schweizer SGS 1-23 for his record-breaking high altitude flight the previous year, was caught out. He had been doing well on his flight and had covered more than 150 miles when a sudden burst of turbulent air forced him down into a narrow mountain valley. He was trying to land in a small sloping field (a difficult enough thing to do even in perfect conditions) when a sudden downdraught caught him and sent him into a high-speed stall. Bill's attempt on the championship ended with a broken back, from which he thankfully recovered, and a glider smashed beyond recognition.

Nicholas and Frank were not put off by what had happened to their friend. They made a good team – and a winning one. Despite a few moments which they brushed off as 'fairly hair-raising'(including gliding home through a pass in the Jura mountains with less than 100ft to spare) they won four of their seven tasks, breaking British records for speed and distance in the process. And, come the end of the week, they were proclaimed the 1956 World Two Seat Gliding Champions.

The local French newspaper – obviously unable to get their tongues around Goodhart and astonished that a competition could be won by such a man in such an undistinguished machine – reported Nicholas's success under a headline: *'Goodears dans sa boite de savon a gagne'* ('Goodears wins in his soapbox'). It was the last time two-seaters featured in a World Championships, so it could be said that Nicholas and Frank are still world champions to this day! Sadly though, Frank did not live to appreciate the irony. He and all his 30 passengers and crew died when the Viscount airliner he was flying was hit in mid-air by an Italian fighter plane on 22nd October 1958.

Soon after getting back from Washington, Nicholas bought a Skylark 3 – the first glider he had ever owned – and once the World Championships were over he was able to set about the task of refining it to competition standard. The Skylark's performance was adequate for competitive flying but its instruments were not, and Nicholas never quite managed to get them to work properly.

The variometer, was particularly temperamental, making it almost impossible for Nicholas to gain height as efficiently as he would have liked while circling in thermals. The idea is that a glider should be flown more slowly in rising air and more quickly when it is sinking – a technique in which the pilot is helped by the *variometer* and a device known as a *MacCready Ring* (a movable scale calibrated to suit the particular type of glider, so that it shows the best speed at which to fly). If the variometer is in any way faulty or badly adjusted, the pilot – even a pilot of Nicholas's ability – cannot know whether he is making the most of the rising air. In a competition this can make the difference between winning and losing.

During his preparation for the 1958 World Championships, a new glider, the Olympia 419, appeared on the scene and Nicholas decided to evaluate it as a possible alternative to his Skylark 3. David Ince, who was acting as test pilot for the manufacturers at the time – takes up the story:

'The first step was a comparative performance test. Early in the day before the thermals started, for these would have totally invalidated our results, we were aerotowed to 5,000ft and cast off together, Nicholas in his Skylark 3 and I in the 419. We started each run or "partial glide" in close formation – both gliders flying at the same speed – until, after an altitude loss in a straight glide of 500ft as measured on my altimeter, we estimated and recorded the height difference between our two gliders. After six runs at progressively increasing speeds, we were running out of height, but the pattern was dramatically clear. In every case the 419 was about five per cent better than the Skylark 3.

'After that, Nicholas had a flight in the 419. Almost certainly he would find the handling superior to anything he had flown before. And what then?'

But he did not choose the 419 for Poland, although he flew it in the following year's Nationals and in the 1960 World Championships in Germany.

In retrospect, it is perhaps easy to understand. For all his instrumentation problems, he was otherwise completely at home in his Skylark 3, which, after almost two years of hard flying, was set up exactly to his liking. The alternative was the second prototype of a new glider scheduled to be ready just three weeks before the team's departure date. The uncertainties were just too great.

Nicholas, in the way he prepared for competitions, was ever a perfectionist. He accepted that seeing and grasping opportunities on the day was what gliding was all about – but he was certainly not prepared to take risks in advance.

On a lighter note, there was his gamesmanship!

As David Ince recalls:

> 'On one competition day, with large cloud amounts and difficult thermalling conditions, it was hard going. Suddenly his confident voice came on the radio, with the faintest hint of laughter: "Nick... approaching Fox..." and giving his altitude.
>
> 'There was utter, unbelieving silence as his fellow competitors looked up, for he was calling from above that murky stuff overhead! Perhaps he was in wave. We could certainly believe it of him with his reputation.
>
> 'Was he hell! He had simply added 5,000 feet to his height! And he continued to do so for the rest of that task. There was much laughter at briefing next day. But Nicholas was quite legal until the Contest Organisation introduced an *ad hoc* rule for the rest of the championships. Radio messages in code were no longer permitted.'

Not surprisingly Nicholas's success as a glider pilot had not gone unnoticed by his Naval superiors, but he would never have expected the letter he received in July 1958 after he finished runner-up – a relative failure, in his estimation – in that year's world championships. It came from Lord Mountbatten of Burma, Prince Philip's uncle who, as First Sea Lord, was head of the Navy and therefore his ultimate boss. Mountbatten wrote:

> *My Dear Goodhart,*
>
> *I send you my best congratulations on your success in the World Gliding Championships in Poland. To come second in the Open Class against the best competition in the world is a magnificent achievement and you must feel very proud.*
>
> *Yours Sincerely,*
>
> *Mountbatten of Burma*

Nicholas would probably have smiled at the idea of getting such top-level acknowledgement for coming a mere second. Winning, not coming second, was what we wanted to do. And winning was something Nicholas was getting rather good at. His competitive nature was ideally suited to the world of competition flying and, once sitting in the cockpit of a glider, there were few to touch him. Over the next 15 years he was British gliding champion three times and a regular member of the British team, flying in seven World Championships, winning one of them, receiving the runner-up prize twice and coming fourth in two of them.

Most men might be satisfied with such an extraordinarily successful record. But not Nicholas. He was never really satisfied with his performance, often rued mistakes he had made and wondered what more he might have achieved had he not made them.

But even he would have been satisfied with what he achieved on 10th May 1959. It was then that Nicholas wrote himself into the record books – as if his achievement of flying higher than any British glider pilot before him was not enough!

It was during the British National Championships at Lasham when pilots were set the task of identifying and then to flying to a specific goal. Thanks to some unhelpfully vague forecasts from the Met Office, Nicholas had no idea where to aim for, so – in a tactic that he later admitted was 'gamesmanship' to confuse the competition – he declared that he would be flying to Portmoak, an airfield on the shores of Loch Leven, just north of Edinburgh, an absurd 400 miles away as the crow (or glider) flew.

He boldly took the first launch in his Skylark 3 at 10.30am – and was back on the ground almost before he knew it. That early in the day the thermals had not yet started building up.

Much chastened, he put his name down for the last launch, waited an hour for his turn, watched his competitors soaring off across the sky – and tried again. And failed again. The tug pilot deposited him into a patch of sinking air, which saw him back on the ground even more quickly than on his first attempt.

Nicholas, normally such a sanguine and optimistic fellow, was thoroughly disheartened and became even more so when, after visiting the clubhouse for some food, he discovered that all his rivals had managed to get away, leaving him virtually the only person still there.

He tried again and, as he trailed behind the tow-plane, he realised that this time it really was third time lucky. The tow-plane was leading him towards a good-looking line of clouds stretching northwards away from the airfield. Clouds like that could mean only one thing; rising air! He released the cable and was on his own, the variometer telling him that he was gaining height at between 5 and 7 knots. He noticed some of the other gliders below him, still circling in their attempt to find a bit of lift. He was back in the game, his enthusiasm rekindled!

Bicester flashed past beneath him, then Birmingham appeared, under a mass of cumulonimbus, sprouting like a giant cauliflower ahead of him. That would mean rain, probably heavy rain, with maybe a bit of thunder and lightning thrown in, but he pushed on, tightening the straps of his harness ready for the inevitable turbulence and switching on the artificial horizon in the cockpit, so he would have a better idea of whether he was flying level when in cloud.

The rain soon turned to hail and was falling so hard he had to slow down to avoid damaging the leading edge of the wings. The noise of it beating on the cockpit was deafening, though not so loud that he could not hear the almost continuous thunder. But thunderstorm or no, he was on his way! Ten thousand feet came and went, so he put on his oxygen mask (oxygen was advisable at that height and would be essential if he got much higher). And then – a blinding flash – as his glider was struck by lightning. The electric shock jerked his legs up so sharply that he cut both his shins deeply on the bottom of the instrument panel.

The hail eased to slush, then to snow, ice began to accumulate on the leading edges of the wings and the Skylark became sluggish, not responding properly to the controls. Nicholas knew it was time to quit.

He turned the glider north and, suddenly, burst out of the impenetrable gloom, with a huge area of England stretched out brightly below him in the brilliant sunshine of an early summer's day, totally at odds with the ice he was carrying on his wings.

In the cockpit, Nicholas still had his problems. He was wet through (glider canopies were not very watertight in those days), his shins were bleeding, his feet were cold and he had little idea where he was.

With ice on its wings, the glider was falling faster than it normally would, but Nicholas calculated he was still high enough to reach another large bank of cloud about 20 miles away and, once there, he would be able to gain enough height for whatever he was going to do next. At 12,000 feet an ice 'log' fell off one of the wings, causing the glider to lurch so violently that the ice was dislodged from the other wing too.

At least now the glider was flying as a glider should...

He entered the next cloud at 5,000 feet and once again hit an impressive core of rising air, which lifted him almost effortlessly back to 15,000 feet. As he emerged back into the sunshine, he saw that a thick mist beneath him was obscuring any view of the ground. He was lost but would press on northwards – in the hope that conditions improved enough for him to land if he had to. Eventually there was land (but what land?) and then what looked like sea (but which sea?). Should he go east or west? And where would either direction take him?

He chose west (a 'half-hearted' decision, he admitted later) and flew on, confident that sooner or later the mist would clear sufficiently for him to get his bearings, which it did – but it was cutting it fine! Eventually, he could see enough of the land to work out that he had ended up a few miles east of Carlisle, but by then he was down to 500 feet – well below the height at which he should have started looking for a field on which to put the glider down. He started scanning the countryside beneath him for a relatively smooth and level landing place – but then felt a wind coming from, of all directions, the southeast. Winds here were not supposed to come from the southeast. Not that he cared. He was down to 300 feet, just above a small ridge. But there was definitely a wind – and it was definitely and unexpectedly coming from the south-east. He turned the glider into it and, to Nicholas's surprise, the little aircraft immediately began to gain height in what was the unmistakable smoothness of rising air. He had been rescued by the Helm Wind, the only wind in the British Isles that has its own name – a violent and unpredictable wind which, at certain times of the year, whistles down the western slopes of the Pennines from the peak of Cross Fell, creating unusually favourable conditions for lost glider pilots who happen to be passing.

He had been at just 300 feet when it started but within minutes was flying at 12,000 feet and rising. He turned the Skylark northward and, as he crossed the Scottish border nine miles north of Carlisle, quickly calculated that he had more than enough height to reach Portmoak – the target he had set purely out of mischievousness but which now, barring disaster, was within reach. An extravagant boast it may have been – but he was going to make it!

And make it he did, although by the time he brought his glider to a halt on that Scottish airfield he was in little mood to celebrate. He was wet, caked in blood and so cold he had lost all feeling in his feet. He didn't have the strength to get out of the cockpit without help.

The flight of 360 miles (579.36 km) had taken him six hours and 23 minutes and established a distance record that stood for 45 years. His average speed of 56.3mph (90.7 kilometres per hour) has never been beaten.

He was asked later how he had done it. Was it luck?

'Yes, of course it was,' he said. 'A whole series of chances came out right.'

In 1972 Nicholas headed for Vršac in Yugoslavia, for the third World Gliding Championships. His plan had been to fly the

Sigma, a revolutionary glider he had designed himself but, when it became clear it would not be ready in time, he looked around for an alternative and was relieved to hear that Slingsby were willing to lend him one of their new Kestrel 19s. He had never flown such a glider before and barely had time to fit it with all the instruments he would need for a major international competition before he joined the other competitors. It was not an ideal way to prepare himself for another assault on the world championship but, in typical form, he made the best of it.

The championships provided some of the most challenging soaring he had attempted to date. On one of the days, Nicholas had two climbs to 19,000ft and on another he reached 17,000ft and 19,000ft. On yet another he climbed to 29,000ft – an extraordinary height for competition flying – and was still ascending at 2,000ft per minute when he broke off the climb, knowing that he was by then more than high enough to complete the task he had been set. At that height he was back in familiar territory, with the bitter cold eating into his body and his feet so numb he hardly knew they were there.

The glider's flaps and ailerons were iced-up and almost immobile and his breath was freezing on the inside of the cockpit canopy so he could barely see out. He had to scrape a hole in the ice so he could take a photograph of the land below him, to prove to the adjudicators that he had indeed reached the turning point required of him.

Even for Nicholas, conditions at Vršac were supremely challenging – but at least he survived. Two pilots were killed before the week was out and two others survived only by baling out after their gliders collided in cloud. Many more failed to reach the airfield at the end of their tasks and had to land out, often in fields which were so brutally rutted or swamped by mud that the retrieve teams took anything up to eight hours to reach the gliders and bring them home. Nicholas Goodhart finished fourth, a remarkable achievement but something of a disappointment for a man as attuned to success as he had become.

He had flown in nine British championships, winning three of them and coming second in another three; he had held 11 British records, one of which still stands to this day; and as a member of the British team had flown in seven world championships, winning once and being runner-up one.

He had been a member of the British Gliding Association Council for many years, served as chairman of its Aerospace Committee, had been awarded the Silver Medal by the Royal Aero Club (in 1956) and the Paul Tissandier Trophy by the FAI, the International Air Sports Federation (in 1972) in recognition of 'those who have served the cause of aviation in general and sporting aviation in particular, by their work, initiative, devotion or in other ways'.

It was a record he could not have dreamed of when, as a teenager, he had watched fascinated as those gliders circled his house at Inkpen. But, although he did not know it as he packed his bags and headed home from Yugoslavia, his gliding career was over.

He was dropped from the British team and – since he flew only for competition – would never get into a glider again. He was, he later admitted, 'a bit miffed' to have his services dispensed with so brutally but he bore the selectors no grudge. He was 53 and knew that a new generation of pilots, who were clearly better than he was at that stage, had to be given their chance.

'They were dead right,' he said later. 'I knew I was over the top.'

Neither did he have any regrets about turning his back on the sport to which he had devoted so much time and energy for more than 35 years. After 20 years as one of the best glider pilots in the world, the idea of 'just flogging around in a glider' held no attraction for him. Without the element of competition, he concluded that gliding would just be 'boring and antisocial'.

So he simply walked away and found something else to do.

7.   Goodhart and the Navy

THE YOUNG MAN WHO JOINED his first ship as a fresh-faced lieutenant in 1940 was well trained, calmly efficient, resourceful and determined to make the most of whatever talents he had been given. But even such an impressive list of attributes gave little indication of the remarkable career that would lie ahead of him. Indeed, Nicholas Goodhart always made out that his entry into the British Senior Service owed as much to good fortune as it did to any driving ambition on his part. If, for example, his father had been able to afford some more conventional public school, he might never have gone to Dartmouth College, which paved his way for entry to the Navy almost before he had thought about it.

And even then it was only the prospect of a modest pay rise that took him into the specialist world of naval flying in which he was to make his name.

'I became an engineer and discovered that life in the engine rooms of ships in those days was pretty rugged,' he said later. 'Hard work. Very hot. No air conditioning or anything like that. And then I discovered you got more pay for going into either flying or into the submarine service – so I volunteered for both.'

Nicholas was famously reticent about his achievements as a Naval officer and preferred simply to describe his career in terms of dates, postings and his rank at the time. Modestly, he brushed off questions about his rise to become Rear Admiral and Companion in The Most Honourable Order of the Bath –

an honour bestowed on him in 1972 for his exemplary naval service. He even suggested that he would have achieved no such success had his superiors not been made aware of his existence by his being court martialled for landing an aeroplane 'wheels-up' in 1949. It was that, he said, that, in the eyes of the Admiralty, marked him out as a man to watch and which helped lift his career to the heights he later achieved.

Not that 'heights' is a word with which he would have been comfortable, no matter how justified it appears to the rest of us. He did write a record of his career, but it was compiled with the utmost economy of detail, drama – and paper! Notable for the total absence of even the slightest bit of self-indulgence (for which he could certainly have been forgiven) and descriptive colour (to which it was genuinely entitled) it read thus:

Hilary Charles Nicholas Goodhart ~ Naval Career

Dec 1940: Emerged from Keyham dressed as a Lieutenant with much book learning but no experience in handling men.

Jan-Mar 1941: Trying to join *HMS Formidable*.

May 1941: Soon after joining *Formidable* we were hit by two 1000lb bombs from Stukas at the evacuation of Crete. Slow return to Alexandria with huge hole in starboard side forward just above waterline. I was given job of organising the repair with a temporary patch. We then sailed for Norfolk Virginia (through the Suez Canal and round Africa) where the US Navy Dockyard carried out a permanent repair.

Oct 1941: Appointed to HMS *Dido* (also under repair in USA but in Brooklyn Navy Yard). We sailed from Brooklyn on Dec 7, 1941 (Pearl Harbour day) for the Mediterranean. Christmas in Malta but spent most of the time in the caves under Valetta as the place was being bombed remorselessly. Then on to Alexandria from where the ship operated for the next two years mainly in support of the Army in North Africa and trying (unsuccessfully) to run convoys to Malta.

Jul 1942: Loaned to HMS *Aldenham* as Chief Engineer Officer (temporary replacement of officer who had gone sick).

Sep 1942: Returned to HMS *Dido*. Continued activity in Eastern Mediterranean. When Rommel kicked out of North Africa, area of operation moved to Algeria, Sicily and Italy.

Nov 1943: Instructed to return to UK for a flying medical.

Jan 1944: Troopship *Louis Pasteur* to Halifax. Flying Training at 13 EFTS St Eugene, Ontario flying Cornells.

Mar 1944: Moved to 31 SFTS Kingston, Ontario flying Harvards. Gained FAA Wings 30/06/44.

Jul 1944: Made my own way to UK.

Aug 1944: Moved to 9 AFU Errol, Perthshire, Scotland flying Masters.

Oct 1944: Moved to 1 NAFS Yeovilton, Somerset flying Wildcats.

Dec 1944: HMS *Smiter* for initial deck landings.

Jan 1945: Hospitalised in RNH Sherborne for an internal op.

April 1945: Appointed to 896 Squadron (Hellcats) to join in Trincomalee. Flew out as passenger in an RAF Liberator. We did not belong to one particular carrier but operated either from *HMS Emperor*, *Ameer* or *Empress* in Indian Ocean for each operation. The task appeared to be mainly clearing up the remnants of the Japanese in Burma and Malaya. Had to ditch in the Malacca Straits due to engine failure. Picked up OK by a destroyer and passed back to the carrier by jackstay.

Sep 1945: Selected for Empire Test Pilots Course starting in Jan '46. Ordered to return to UK immediately to do a Seafire conversion course in order to build up my hours (only 407 at this point). Returned to UK from Colombo in a York (passenger version of the Lancaster) Not a very reliable aeroplane.

Oct 1945: Seafire course at St Merryn.

Jan 1946: Joined No.4 course at ETPS Cranfield. This was a 5 month course rather than the normal year. Types flown: Tiger Moth. Harvard, Firefly, Spitfire, Tempest, Oxford, Mosquito, Meteor, Lancaster.

Jun 1946: Senior pilot of 700 squadron at Yeovilton teaching Maintenance Test Flying to Navy Pilots. Types flown: Harvard, Barracuda, Firefly, Seafire, Master, Tiger Moth, Sea Otter, Firebrand.

Mar 1948: Donibristle Naval Aircraft Repair Yard as Maintenance Test Pilot. Types flown: Tiger Moth, Dominie, Seafire, Oxford, Harvard, Firefly.

Jun 1948: Intensive Flying Development Flight at Boscombe Down. Types flown: Seafire, Meteor, Sea Fury, Prentice, Sea Hornet, Oxford, Dominie, Firefly, Tiger Moth, Seafang, Heston, Vampire.

Oct 1948: 'C' Squadron at Boscombe Down. Types flown (in addition to those listed for 1FDF): Firebrand, Sea Vampire, Trent Meteor, Wyvern 1, Sturgeon, Sea Meteor, Hawker N7, Mamba Balliol, Ercoupe.

Aug 1949: By RMS *Queen Mary* to New York. Exchange test pilot in Flight Test at US Naval Air Test Center, Patuxent River.

Types flown: SNB, F8F, XTB3F, F9F, F4U, SNJ, F2H, AD, F-84, XF3D.

Jan 1950: By RMS *Queen Elizabeth* to Southampton. Rejoined 'C' Squadron. Further types flown: Attacker, Sea Prince, Wyvern 2.

Aug 1950: Technical Secretary to Chief Naval Representative at the Ministry of Supply.

May 1951: Loaned to Westlands to assist with production testflying of Wyverns.

Sep 1951: Returned to Technical Secretary Duties.

Jan 1953: Promoted Commander. By RMS *Queen Elizabeth* to New York. Staff Air Engineer Officer and Staff Pilot, British Joint Services Mission, Washington DC. Types flown: SNB, Sea Prince, Heron, T-33, Otter and numerous American gliders and private aircraft.

Dec 1955: By RMS *Queen Mary* to Southampton. Air Engineer Officer, RNAS Yeovilton. Types flown: Sea Vampire, Meteor, Seafire, Sea Venom, Sea Prince.

Jan 1958: Naval Air Warfare Division, Admiralty.

Nov 1959: Helicopter Conversion Course at RNAS Culdrose.

Feb 1960: Staff of Flag Officer Aircraft Carriers at SAEO and SMEO. Variously embarked in HM Ships Ark Royal, Victorious and Hermes.

Feb 1962: Promoted Captain. Ministry of Aviation as Project Manager of Sea Dart missile.

Jan 1965: Student at Imperial Defence College.

Jan 1966: Hunter Conversion Course at RNAS Brawdy.

Feb 1966: Director of Aircraft Maintenance and Repair, Admiralty.

Feb 1968: Promoted Commodore. Deputy Director of Operational Requirements at Ministry of Defence.

Jul 1970: Promoted Rear Admiral. Military Deputy to Head of Defence Sales at Ministry of Defence.

Apr 1973: Retired.

And that, in the no-nonsense style of Nicholas Goodhart, was that. All essential facts, relevant dates and places recorded accurately. Nothing missing. What more could you want?

This was a man who never looked back, neither in pride nor in anger. What's done is done; what's next? That remained his philosophy until the day he died.

If you pressed him sufficiently to acknowledge that his long military career was truly exceptional he would do no more than nod and tell you: 'One did what one did.'

The Royal Navy itself is not much help to anyone hoping to learn more of the dedicated and distinguished 37-year career of Rear Admiral H.C.N. Goodhart CB. The Military brooks no sentiment and when that career came to an end the announcement from the Naval Secretary stuck to the facts:

> 'No further employment will be available for Rear Admiral H.C.N. Goodhart CB after he has relinquished the appointment of Military Deputy to Head of Defence Sales and the First Sea Lord has therefore approved that he should be placed on the Retired List to date 7 April 1973 having had 28 days Terminal Leave and 28 days pre-release vocational training from 10 February to 6 April 1973.'

The announcement, dated 12th December 1972, was accompanied by an equally economical, hyperbole-free account of his Record of Service:

Entered Royal Navy 1 May 1936

Promoted Sub Lieutenant 16 April 1939

Promoted Lieutenant 16 December 1940

Promoted Lieutenant Commander 16 December 1948

Promoted Commander 30 June 1952

Promoted Captain 30 June 1962

Promoted Rear Admiral 7 July 1970

The final entry necessarily employed a few more words:

Appointed Commander of the Most Honourable Order of the Bath – Birthday Honours 1972.

A civilian account of that Record of Service might have contained a few more words; employed some colour, registered some pride but that would not have suited the subject of it one little bit. That's the way it was done. And that would have been just fine by Nicholas Goodhart.

Naturally a stickler for doing things 'properly' and a stranger to gratuitous emotion he was very much at home in an environment which did not encourage departure from those 'qualities'. Indeed, his service records reveal a curt slapping down from above for a Captain Nigel Bailey who, in 1958, gave the rising Commander Goodhart a glowing reference.

Captain Bailey wrote:

'He is employed as my Technical Assistant and his knowledge and advice in this sphere is sound and all embracing. He has a quick and inventive brain and is always forthcoming with ideas for the future. He is an able and trusted Staff officer of the highest calibre. Devoted to the Service he interests himself in all aspects of Marine and Aviation engineering. A loyal Staff officer with a great charm of manner and a cheerful disposition. A glider pilot of international reputation. An officer well fitted for the higher ranks for which he is recommended.'

That splendid assessment was accompanied, under Section Two, by marks out of ten for: Professional ability (8); Mental qualities (9); Personal qualities (8) and Administrative qualities (8) and signed with a flourish by Captain Nigel Bailey, Royal Navy.

However, Vice Admiral L.G. Durlacher, the Senior Officer who signed off Captain Bailey's report, was singularly unimpressed by the assessor's enthusiasm. Complaining that Captain Bailey was in the habit of 'over-marking', the Vice Admiral, while admitting that he barely knew Goodhart, added:

'However, I doubt whether he is as good as the assessments in Section Two indicate and taking into consideration Captain Bailey's tendency to over-mark I have amended these assessments. I have applied an Index Error of -1 because of the standard of marking of Captain Bailey.'

There is, of course, no record of Captain Bailey's response to the dismissive Vice Admiral Durlacher when Goodhart subsequently rose to the rank of Rear Admiral but it's nice to imagine that it would have been a two fingered salute and a warm glow of satisfaction!

Vice Admiral Durlacher's reluctance to accept the rave reviews of Goodhart was certainly not shared by Rear Admiral Smeeton who signed off an assessment by Captain Hallett in 1961.

Captain Hallett had declared Goodhart '...an excellent staff Air Engineer and Engineer Officer who has proved to be an asset in every way.' And there was no marking down from Rear Admiral Smeeton who concurred, adding that Goodhart was:

> '...an outstandingly able Engineer Officer who does not spare himself in his work. He has a strong character and a very pleasant personality. He is decisive and sound in his judgment and completely loyal to the best interests of the Service. He shows fine qualities of leadership and is popular with all ranks. I recommend him for immediate promotion.'

Indeed, with only the occasional rebuke for being impetuous, a tad arrogant at times, sometimes impatient in his dealings with civilian staff and, of course, that Court Martial verdict, Goodhart's assessments throughout the years of his Royal Navy service were glowing and exemplary and all the more remarkable and impressive given that as a young man he had no particular desire or aptitude for a Naval career.

There's a quotation from Oliver Cromwell, which perhaps sums it up very nicely: *'No man goes further than he who knows not where he is going.'*

Nicholas Goodhart knew not where he was going when he entered Dartmouth Royal Naval College, aged 13. But few had gone further when he came to the end of that voyage. And what a career it was! Best described, perhaps, in the understated list to be found under: *'Principal Appointments of Rear Admiral H.C.N. Goodhart CB'.*

War Service
1939-1945: HM Ships *Formidable* and *Dido*.

As Commander
1952-54: Staff Air Engineering Officer to the Admiral British Joint Services Mission, Washington.

1954-55: Duty with Technical Services (Ministry of Supply) in British Joint Services Mission, Washington.

1956-58: Royal Naval Air Station Yeovilton as Air Engineering Officer.

1958-60: Duty with Director of Air Warfare, Admiralty.

1960-62: Staff of Flag Officer Aircraft Carriers as Staff Engineer Officer and Staff Air Engineer Officer.

As Captain

1962-64: Assistant Director, Guided Weapons (Naval) in Ministry of Aviation 1965: Course at Imperial Defence College.

1966-67: Director of Aircraft Maintenance and Repair of the staff of Director General Aircraft (Naval) 1967-68: Director of Aircraft Engineering (Naval) on the staff of Director General Aircraft (Naval)

1968-69: Deputy to Deputy Chief of the Defence Staff (Operational Requirements) and Director of Defence Operational Requirements Staff (in the rank of Commodore)

As Rear Admiral

1970-73 Military Deputy to the Head of Defence Sales in the Ministry of Defence.

His Record of Service in the Royal Navy reads:

Entered Royal Navy: 1 May 1936

Promoted Sub Lieutenant: 16 April 1939

Promoted Lieutenant: 16 December 1940

Promoted Lieutenant Commander: 16 December 1948

Promoted Commander: 30 June 1952

Promoted Captain 30 June 1962

Promoted Rear Admiral 7 July 1970

Appointed Commander of the Most Honourable Order of the Bath: Birthday Honours List 1972.

The appraisals, held by the Ministry of Defence, of Goodhart's progress through the ranks make fascinating reading:

1941: In this his first ship as a Watchkeeping Engineer Officer he has on the whole carried out his duties satisfactorily but he could set himself a higher standard and display more apparent interest in practical marine engineering and he has still to learn a greater sense of responsibility.

1943: This officer has a very quick and active brain and a technical knowledge well above average. He can assimilate facts very quickly but is inclined to be too hasty in forming his conclusions. He can be relied on to get things done quickly and efficiently and is a very capable organiser but needs to show a little more tact at times to get the best out of his men.

1950: This officer has exceptional knowledge of aviation, its science and technicalities. His intellect is extremely keen and his judgement very sound. His personality is strong and his manner and appearance very presentable. He expresses himself forthrightly and candidly in conversation, sometimes at the expense of tact, but he is less effectual on paper.

1960: An outstandingly able Engineer Officer who does not spare himself in his work. He has a strong character and a very pleasant personality. He is incisive and sound in his judgment and completely loyal to the best interests of the Service. He shows fine qualities of leadership and is popular with all ranks. I recommend him for immediate promotion.

1961: I am even more convinced that the Royal Navy will be the loser if Goodhart is not promoted to the higher ranks of the Service. He is in every way an exceptionally outstanding and gifted officer whose talents we simply cannot afford to lose.

1968: An officer of undoubted intelligence and ability, he has an alert manner and a probing inquisitiveness which is always seeking better ways of doing things and of improving what we have. He is forceful in argument but has a good judgment and a wide appreciation of staff and planning problems. He has the potential for Flag Rank.

Accolades abound in the Goodhart personal file, but one stands out from the others. It is a memorandum to the Ministry of Defence in London from Lieutenant General T.R. Milton, United States Air Force, Vice Director, International Military Staff and Chairman of the NATO MC Group of Experts. It reads:

> 'It is my pleasure to bring to your attention the outstanding performance of duty of Commodore H C N Goodhart RN, while acting as a member of the NATO Military Committee Group of Automatic Data Processing Experts during the period 15 July 1969 to 1 October 1969.
>
> 'The Group of Experts was tasked with the difficult and exacting assignment of examining the existing Military Committee arrangements for control and direction of Automatic Data Processing developing in support of Military Command, Control and Information Systems throughout NATO, making recommendations for such changes deemed necessary to improve current organisation and outlining the general principles for

military automatic data processing development in NATO to support the military command and control functions of the international and national headquarters of the Alliance.

'By virtue of the superior abilities of Commodore Goodhart the task was completed ahead of the scheduled termination date in an expert and professional manner. The report exceeds in all respects the terms of reference provided and lays the groundwork for the development and acquisition of an improved NATO Military Command. Commodore Goodhart's comprehensive and expert knowledge of both the military command and the control environment and of the potential of effective Automatic Data Processing support was a key element in the success of the Group of Experts.

'Commodore Goodhart's outstanding performance of duty has reflected great credit upon himself, the North Atlantic Treaty Organisation and his nation.'

It could be argued that it had taken the Royal Navy rather a long time to recognise fully and reward appropriately the extraordinarily varied and versatile talents of Goodhart but by 1962 the military top brass appeared, at least, to have become properly aware and appreciative of his remarkably inventive mind when, on his promotion to Captain, the Ministry of Aviation appointed him Project Manager of Sea Dart missile.

Here, he worked for three years with Hawker Siddeley on designing a new missile to protect the Royal Navy surface fleet. Trials of the missile started in 1965 and orders were placed by the Ministry of Defence in 1967. It reflects enormous credit on all concerned with its successful development, particularly in the early stages, to record that Sea Dart went on to have a long life in active service. It was still proving its worth in the Falklands War in 1982, downing seven Argentine aircraft, and a decade later in the 1991 Gulf War, when *HMS Gloucester* shot down an Iraqi Silkworm missile as it headed for what would have been a disastrous strike on the American battleship USS Missouri. It was the first time that a missile had shot down another missile.

For an extraordinary 40 years Sea Dart remained the Royal Navy's principal shield against air attack until, as reported with brilliant, evocative pictures in the magazine *Navy News,* its retirement was celebrated with a roaring final flourish off Scotland. The magazine recorded how Sea Dart missiles were fired by a Royal Navy warship for the last time on April 20, 2012:

> 'HMS *Edinburgh* launched seven of the Mach 2 missiles at target drones off the Outer Hebrides in a last hurrah ahead of a major military exercise off western Scotland.'

Sadly, Nicholas Goodhart, one of the Sea Dart pioneers, died a year before its historic farewell but, in any event, he would have been far more interested in what was going to replace it!

Goodhart's insatiable enthusiasm for all things new was also put to good use by the military top brass when, on promotion to Rear Admiral in 1970, he was appointed Deputy to the Head of Defence Sales at the Ministry of Defence.

Here, he was effectively a high class, high powered salesman selling British made guns, tanks, ships, submarines and aircraft to other countries – travelling to wherever an inquiry from a foreign power took him, often aboard the Royal Fleet auxiliary ship HMS *Tarbetness*, which was equipped like a floating shop so that prospective purchasers could see the British military wares on offer without having to leave their own shores.

Included among the countries with which Nicholas was responsible for business were Peru, Chile, Argentina, Brazil, Venezuela, Columbia, Japan and Iran, whose Navy acquired a new British submarine. He continued in that fascinating role, with its exciting worldwide travel and top level wheeler-dealing, for three years until he retired from the Royal Navy in 1973.

Typically, that 'retirement' was very short-lived. It lasted only a couple of months before he was appointed consultant to the giant American Boeing Aircraft Company, looking after their military interests in London. This was a natural progression from the top class international sales job he had done for the Ministry of Defence – the difference being that he was now tasked with interesting *them* in buying from *him*.

In this role, Nicholas was responsible for the British Armed Forces' acquisition of two hugely significant Boeing products – selling the hydrofoil HMS *Speedy* to the Royal Navy and the Chinook helicopter to the Royal Air Force.

Rear Admiral H.C.N. Goodhart (Retd) had thrown himself into this civilian job with his customary enthusiasm – the exciting, ground breaking Speedy and Chinook appealing hugely to his natural instincts as an inventor, inherited from his father (who had so indulged impecunious like-minded associates in the 1920s and '30s) and pursued with passion (not to mention a good deal more success!) throughout his own life.

He was responsible for persuading the Royal Navy to purchase the Boeing Jetfoil, a waterjet propelled hydrofoil. The objective was to use HMS *Speedy* to establish the technical and performance capabilities of hydrofoil craft under military conditions and to assess its potential for fishery protection duties.

HMS *Speedy*, a 119-tonne jetfoil built by Boeing in Seattle and fitted out in Portsmouth with much British equipment aboard, was ordered by the Labour Government in 1979 and launched in Seattle by Mrs Margaret Jay, wife of the then ambassador to the United States in June of that year. The Navy then set about operational evaluation of *Speedy* in what was called the *offshore tapestry role* – fishery and oil rig protection.

While the Royal Navy and the relevant Labour ministers had apparently been satisfied by that evaluation, HMS *Speedy* was terminated by the Conservative Government in 1982, leading to a House of Commons bust-up over the alleged 'unseemly haste' of that decision.

Paradoxically, while the short-lived HMS *Speedy* had been a relatively easy 'sell' to an enthusiastic British government, for Nicholas Goodhart, selling the Chinook helicopter – which was to prove a tremendously successful and enduring acquisition – was very hard work.

Initially there was little or no interest from the Ministry of Defence in this revolutionary helicopter and it took three years of typical Goodhart obstinacy and persistence to get the politicians to recognise the aircraft's immense worth. Unlike them, of course, Nicholas had flown military machines and fought wartime aerial battles. He had flown in Chinooks in America and was convinced of their potential. He simply would not give up. He was determined to wear down the government's resistance and, when all else looked like failing, he took the Chinook to his contacts among the RAF top brass, where the helicopter's capabilities could be assessed in a spirit of mutual military respect. They were thrilled, thought it a fantastic prospect and agreed to join Nicholas in his mission to overturn the politicians' lack of interest.

Finally, it worked. The RAF acquired Chinooks and, later, so did the Army. The iconic helicopter went on to become an important part of Britain's defence capability, to this day serving with distinction in Afghanistan, saving countless lives and being flown famously by Prince William.

Nicholas Goodhart worked successfully looking after Boeing's British military interests for seven years, until finally ending his own connection with the Armed Forces in 1980.

It had been an association spanning well over 40 years.

But still there was no place for the word 'retirement' in the Goodhart vocabulary and his civilian business interests were to endure until his death in 2011.

8.   Goodhart the life-saver

IT WAS A YOUNG WOMAN with a make-up mirror who helped Nicholas Goodhart become a legend in naval flying. It was in 1950 and Nicholas – by then Technical Secretary to the Chief Naval Representative in the Ministry of Supply – had long been troubled by the number of good pilots being lost while attempting landings on aircraft carriers.

Landing on a carrier was a tricky business, even for the best of pilots, partly because of the small landing area they had to aim for and partly because of the unpredictable movement of the carrier on the sea beneath them as they approached. If pilots made even the slightest miscalculation, they could land too short and crash into the ship, or too long and crash into the sea – and this was happening far too often.

During the war, the high rate of deck landing accidents had been more or less accepted as inevitable but in the post-war years much thought was being given as to how to reduce it, especially as there had been no improvement in the equipment used on ships to cater for the faster and heavier planes now landing on them.

The admiralty were even beginning to think that, in the interests of safety, limits would have to be put on the design and development of naval aircraft until something was done to make the carriers' landing systems better able to cope with them.

It was a big problem and one which put pilots' lives at risk every time they came in to land on a carrier at sea. But nobody in the highest echelons of either the Royal or the US Navy seemed to have the faintest idea how to do anything about it.

Enter Nicholas Goodhart. As one of the few naval officers who knew as much about flying as he did about ships, he was well placed to solve the problem. And it was just the sort of challenge that he revelled in. As he put it:

> 'In those days we used to make a horizontal approach coupled with a clever dive at the deck at the last minute – followed by a beautifully judged flare to avoid breaking the undercarriage, like a piece of ballet dancing. A roar of applause, great success, and everybody thought it was wonderful. The trouble was a lot of people couldn't do it, and even the best of chaps could not do it right all the time and the accident rate was terribly high.'

The system being used at that time required a deck landing control officer standing amidships on the port side and using two bats to signal to the incoming pilot, telling him what corrections to make as he approached the ship. It was a method that was almost as dangerous as it was unsophisticated – and one that became a recipe for chaos when American aircraft came to land on British ships, or British ones on American ships, since some of the signals employed by Royal Navy 'batsmen' meant precisely the opposite of those used by their counterparts in the US Navy.

Nicholas believed that the dangers of landing on carriers were exacerbated by the steep final approaches applicable at that time, which made the flare even more critical and more difficult to achieve.

Obviously, he realised, an aircraft carrier was too short for these new high performance jets to flare and drift down onto the deck as they would do on an airfield. Nicholas thought that a constant and shallower approach path, all the way to touch down, would eliminate the need to flare without too great an impact as the plane hit the deck. It would require precise flying and, somehow, account would have to be taken of the motion of the ship, but he was positive it could be done.

All he had to do was provide a means of enabling pilots to fly the more gentle approach path with sufficient accuracy to make a firm and positive arrival within 50 feet of the desired landing point. So it was this upon which he focused his attention.

He knew that from time immemorial, seamen navigating in narrow channels had been using *leading marks* – easily identifiable features on the land or fixed to buoys on the sea – which sailors at the helm had to keep in the right position relative to the ship and to each other if the rocks were to be avoided.

Pilots landing on an aircraft carrier faced exactly the same problem but in the vertical rather than the horizontal plane, so it seemed natural to consider how the principle could be adapted for use in carriers.

A few problems were immediately apparent.

The first was that leading marks are more accurate the further they are apart – and on an aircraft carrier, even if one light is right on the bow and the other right at the stern, they can be no further apart than the length of the ship.

The second problem was that leading marks need to be above the observer's skyline if they are to be properly visible – and that would simply not be possible for a pilot flying towards a ship.

Even worse, Nicholas realised, the pitching of the ship would move the defined line up and down, making it impossible for the pilot to follow. And in any case, since any deck landing arrangement would have to be equally useful for day and night flying, it would have to involve lights, not just marks.

In the face of so many problems, other people might have given up and agreed that the only answer was to put a brake on the development of aircraft, which were too fast and heavy for the carriers then in service. But Nicholas knew he was onto something and was not going to be deflected from it. It soon became clear that there was no practical way of using something as simple as two leading lights to do the job, but what if he used a mirror with a light shining onto it from a different part of the ship? That, surely, would have the desired effect.

Nicholas decided on a vertical mirror whose midpoint would be defined by green lights on either side. It would be positioned to reflect a bright light shone from the carrier's stern, so that all a pilot had to do was maintain the required approach speed and keep the reflected blob of light in the middle of the mirror in line with the green lights at the side. If the bright light fell below the green ones he was flying too low; if it went above it he was flying too high. To cope with the up and down movement of the ship, the mirror would be adjustable on a horizontal axis, with a gyro-stabilisation system to ensure that the flight path was always at the required angle to the horizontal.

The idea was clear in Nicholas's mind. He was sure it would work. But it was one thing to have had the idea and quite another to get anything done about it.

It was Nicholas's good fortune that his immediate superior at that time was Captain Dennis Campbell, the Deputy Chief Naval Representative, whose duties included advising the Ministry of Supply on research and development as it pertained to the operation of aircraft from ships. Campbell had a large model aircraft carrier in his office and one day, while he was out at lunch, Nicholas used it to put his idea to the test.

With the connivance of Miss Montgomery, his boss's secretary, he conducted the practical experiment, which would show beyond doubt that he had invented something very significant indeed.

He first persuaded Miss Montgomery to part with her powder compact, then drew a line across the middle of its mirror with her lipstick. They set the mirror up on the port side of the flight deck on the Captain's model and placed a torch on the stern. Then, with Miss Montgomery despatched to the far end of the room, Nicholas adjusted the tilt of the mirror until she could see the reflection of the torchlight exactly on the lipstick line. He then told her to walk towards the model, crouching down more and more as she went so that she always kept the reflection on the line of lipstick. When her chin came to rest on the stern of the model's flight deck Miss Montgomery had successfully completed the first *mirror deck* landing.

Nicholas's *mirror deck landing system* underwent initial trials on HMS *Indomitable*, former flagship of the Home Fleet, before undergoing further tests at Boscombe Down and on HMS *Illustrious*.

At each stage of the process, the life-saving potential of the invention became more apparent. It was adjudged to halve the risk of human error when landing on an aircraft carrier and made it possible for pilots to pay less attention to the ship they were landing on and to concentrate instead on ensuring that the lights shining on the mirror ahead of them were in the right position.

The device was introduced by the Royal Navy in 1954, by the US Navy in 1955 and by the navy of every nation on earth that had aircraft carriers soon afterwards. It reduced the accident rate on Royal Navy aircraft carriers by a factor of 18 and, for US carriers, it was recorded that the accident rate fell from 35 per 10,000 landings in 1954 to seven per 10,000 landings in 1957. It was also reckoned to have saved the US Navy around £7 million a year.

It is little surprise that in appreciation of this achievement, the US Navy awarded Nicholas the Legion of Merit.

His invention attracted the attention of the British quality press and one of them – probably *The Times* – recorded under the headline *RN's Mirrors Save U.S. $7m A Year*:

> 'The British-invented mirror landing system which the United States now uses on board its aircraft carriers was credited today with saving the American Navy £7 million a year. This was because the accident rate in carrier landings had dropped from 2.4 per thousand to 0.98
>
> 'Another contributory factor in this improvement was the British-invented angled deck on carriers. At the Patuxent naval base, Maryland, today the use of the mirror landing system was demonstrated for the first time to the public, though it has been in use in some American carriers for a year or two.
>
> 'A Naval spokesman said the device would shortly be installed on 14 more carriers and on runways at 60 naval air stations. Through the use of the mirror system the pilot can make a precise landing at a pre-determined point.
>
> 'A large curved mirror mounted on the port side of the flight deck is the pilot's target as he approaches for landing. By focusing on a brilliant spot of light reflected in the mirror the pilot provides himself with an optical glide path that guides him to the deck. The mirror system has replaced the officer who guided planes in by waving signal 'bats'.'

9. Goodhart the inventor

ALTHOUGH THE MIRROR DECK landing system was the most high profile and undoubtedly the most successful of his inventions, it was by no means the only device dreamed up by the ingenious mind of Nicholas Goodhart. He was as single-minded in his pursuit of better ways of doing things as he was in every other aspect of his life. As he himself put it:

> 'If I happen on a system or device where the current solution seems clumsy, inadequate or too extensive – or fails to take advantage of current technical knowledge – I feel a strong urge to explore the possibilities to see what I think could be done to better meet the requirement. Even worse, one occasionally comes across a gap where there obviously could be a system or device to fill it, but none exists. This has happened many times.'

That is not to say that all his ideas were seized on by a grateful world. Sometimes they were dismissed as unnecessary, unworkable or just plain cranky – but he put this down to the short-sightedness of his critics rather than to any shortcomings in his creative skills.

In the early 1950s, for example, at about the same time as his mirror deck landing system was beginning to save lives on the world's aircraft carriers, he came up with an idea which, he was convinced, would be the answer to many of the traffic jams that were building up on our roads. He had always been interested in traffic (how it flowed and, more interestingly to him, how it sometimes did not) so he put his mind to the problem of congestion around roundabouts.

Nicholas could never quite understand why the roundabout – a device intended to ease the flow of traffic at busy road junctions – frequently had precisely the opposite effect. It did not take him long to realise that the problem was caused by the rule of the road, which decreed that traffic already on the roundabout should give way to the traffic entering it. This had the effect that a continuous stream of traffic entering from any of the feeder roads quickly brought the circulation to a stand-still.

To Nicholas the solution was as obvious as the problem. Change the rule of the road. But that would have been a problem in its own right. The population of Britain may seem slow to accept change these days but, compared with those early post-war days, people now are flexible beyond degree.

Nicholas wrote to the Ministry of Transport, explaining the problem and proposing his solution. He didn't even get a reply!

Although he was typically confident in his idea, he was realistic enough to accept that even a man as dogged as he was unlikely to change the closed minds of the Whitehall bureaucrats, so he forgot all about it. But when, a couple of years later, the *Daily Telegraph* wrote about the increasing problem of gridlock in busy cities, Nicholas dusted down his old idea, modified it just a little and sent it to the newspaper's columnist with his best wishes.

The problem, so the newspaper had said, arose at crossroads, when heavy traffic meant that motorists attempting to go straight ahead were unable to exit the junction, thus blocking it in all directions.

Nicholas's solution was simple. The area in the middle of the crossroads should be painted with yellow cross-hatchings and drivers should be forbidden to drive onto it unless they could get out the other side. The *Daily Telegraph* columnist wrote back and said that it was a stupid idea, asserting that nobody would take the least notice of the cross-hatchings and that painting them on the road would simply be a waste of money.

A few years later the Ministry of Transport put forward an idea they called the *box junction* – in which yellow cross-hatching was used to indicate areas into which drivers should not proceed unless their exit was clear on the other side. In later life Nicholas jokingly laid claim to having invented the box junction, although in more honest moments he conceded that he had simply thought of it years before some 'lackey' at the DoT had come up with the system we see in use on our roads today.

Other inventions weren't even a success with his family, let alone the wider world, but that didn't stop him trying. Once, while visiting his step-daughter Alyson and her husband (journalist Simon Hoggart) in America he had what he considered the brainwave idea of a device that would keep tonic water fresh by squeezing the air out of the plastic bottles in which it was contained. 'He gave up when the thing had reached a size only slightly smaller than a wardrobe,' Simon recalled later.

Nicholas's mechanised corkscrew was not much better, although his family did agree that it might have worked – if it had not weighed roughly twice as much as the bottle of wine it was supposed to open!

Nicholas's inventing prowess, not unnaturally, spread into his flying activities too. Some of his gliding friends were surprised to find him in his cockpit with a bizarre contraption which looked like (and in fact was) a piece of knicker elastic fixed to an old ruler. This, he explained, was his invention for establishing where he should be on the map on any particular flight, taking into account such vagaries as wind speed, wind direction, ground speed and time. With this simple device he could work out precisely where he should be at any given time and at what time he should arrive at his intended destination.

The device worked splendidly, and so did the slightly more sophisticated plastic model he made when he realised knicker elastic was not quite right for a production model, and he was seriously tempted to take out a patent.

'But then I thought, *why should I bother to deal with plastic manufacturers and patents and all that?*' he said later. 'The one I had made was all I needed, so I dropped the whole thing and got on with the many other aspects of my life. And that was pretty much the story behind a whole lot of ideas and inventions which came up as time went by. My enjoyment lay in inventing, not in managing and marketing, which is boring and time consuming.'

After so much success as a glider pilot it was no surprise that one of Nicholas Goodhart's most important 'inventions' was an aircraft which would – he hoped – bring him even more.

He had long dreamed of using the knowledge of aircraft design he had gained as a test pilot and combining it with his experience as a competitive glider pilot to come up with a plane that would leave the rest of the gliding world trailing in its slipstream, so when in 1966 the British Gliding Association started putting together a team to design and build a world-beating glider, his was probably the first name on the list.

The BGA's plan was to bring together some of the best brains from the British gliding fraternity to design and build a new experimental aircraft with the single intention of winning the open class of the World Gliding Championships scheduled for Marfa in Texas in 1970.

The BGA wanted to 'deliver to a British pilot selected to compete in the World Championships, a system having the highest probability enabling him to win, within the limitations of finance that may be raised to achieve this aim.'

The success of the project would depend on three essentials – finding the right man to take technical charge, giving him the necessary resources to get the job done, and tapping into the accumulated expertise of anyone else with the required technical specialist knowledge.

The first part – finding the right man to lead to team – was easily achieved. Once Nicholas Goodhart had expressed an interest there was no need for further debate. He already had some of the answers, if only in his head.

Working with Nicholas would be some of the biggest names in gliding, including George Burton (a leading pilot who was soon to become managing director of one of the country's biggest glider building companies), Ken Wilkinson (another fine glider pilot who ended his career as managing director of British Airways), Beverley Shenstone (who had designed two other gliders and was responsible for the extraordinary elliptical wing of the Spitfire) together with Frank Irving (senior aeronautics lecturer at Imperial College in charge of the wind tunnels used in the design) and Lorne Welch (who had been held in Colditz Castle as a prisoner of war, and who advised on the design of *The Colditz Cock* – the glider the prisoners there secretly made for an escape attempt). Irving and Welch, among many other achievements, had in 1955 become the first pilots to cross the English Channel in a two-seat glider. Last, but certainly not least, was Mike Gee – the financial brains behind it all.

The BGA would have ultimate responsibility for the project, with financial backing coming from British industry and –

ultimately – the Ministry of Defence, which later took it on as a research project, but nobody doubted that it was Nicholas who was in charge and who would demand full technical responsibility as the work went on.

The team recognised that to become the best glider in the world the Sigma, as it was called, would have to be radically different. Conventional gliders, it was accepted, had always been something of a compromise – between what was best for high-speed flying (essential when cruising between thermals) and what was needed for circling at low speed in the rising air of thermals.

This new British glider would put an end to such compromise by incorporating all manner of new ideas – not least a pair of wings whose major characteristics could be adjusted in flight. When circling in thermals the wing area and camber could be increased and the aspect ratio reduced, so the glider could fly more slowly, helping the rate of climb. But when flying between thermals the wing area and camber could be reduced and the aspect ratio increased, thus improving the penetration.

The idea was not entirely new. Sigma would not be the first glider to aim for such remarkable engineering (a German aircraft had shown similar, though not so advanced, thinking at the 1967 World Championships in South Cerney) but Nicholas was convinced it would be possible to take the existing technology to so far undreamed of levels of sophistication. He made it clear that, while 'a large amount of ingenuity' would be required, he did not intend to use unconventional methods where established ones were already good enough.

The aim, he said, would have to be a balance between designing and building a first class aircraft and doing everything possible to ensure maximum pilot efficiency. Being a successful glider pilot himself, Nicholas knew that winning a championship depended on a good deal more than the performance capabilities of the aircraft. Nevertheless, while everything had to be taken into account – from the comfort of the pilot to the ease of any necessary repairs, for example – he insisted that the design of the aircraft had to come first. 'No matter how good the pilot or those other considerations are, they will not compensate for a poorly-performing glider,' he said.

The project would involve not just the glider itself but its instrumentation and its trailer – and there was an agreement that if the design turned out to be as successful as they believed it would, the drawings would be made available so that the Sigma could go fully into production.

Work on the Sigma Project began in 1966, with the prototype being built at the long established Slingsby glider factory at Kirkbymoorside in North Yorkshire.

It was to be a glider like no other.

The team decided that the aircraft would have a stiff 21-metre wing made, for the purpose of adding strength, of aluminium alloy rather than the more usual and more aerodynamically efficient glass-fibre, which was becoming more commonly used by gliders at that time.

With a complicated system of flaps that could emerge from inside the high-aspect-ratio wings, the area could be increased by 35 per cent to allow the Sigma to circle very efficiently in thermals on cross-country flights.

It was expected that the design would make the Sigma about 15 per cent faster than the best of its more conventional rivals when flying cross-country and, based on analysis of the nature of thermals, they reasoned that once the flaps were deployed to increase the wing area, the Sigma would be able to circle so slowly it could gain maximum benefit by staying close to the central (and strongest) part of the thermal.

Nobody doubted that it was a design that should – and almost certainly would – work and with the new glider beginning to take shape there was an air of real excitement, both among the men building it and in the gliding fraternity much further afield.

But unfortunately the Sigma project was to suffer a major setback when, on 18th November 1968 – with the research phase completed and the construction of the first prototype just begun – a disastrous fire destroyed the factory, including all the hardware being used on the Sigma, all the jigs and nearly all the drawings.

It was a blow from which the project never fully recovered, although the BGA – showing remarkable if misplaced optimism – said they were confident that the Sigma would still be finished and ready to compete in the 1970 World Gliding Championships.

But for the fire, the Sigma would have been nearing its first flight sometime in 1969 but when the Duke of Edinburgh – one of the project's biggest supporters – visited the factory on 6th February the new post-fire prototype was only just beginning to take shape. Things took a further turn for the worse just five months later when Slingsby went into liquidation and the entire project had to be moved to Cranfield in Bedfordshire.

In addition, there was no denying that doubts were beginning to emerge. Was the alloy the right material with which to construct the wing? Were the hinges on the flaps making the glider aerodynamically inefficient? Was it asking for too much physical effort from the pilot to expect him to repeatedly pump the pedals to operate the hydraulics? Relatively small problems but cumulatively enough to make some people wonder whether Sigma would ever get off the ground.

However, on the evening of Saturday 26th July 1971, the first Sigma glider was rolled out from the workshops of the BEA Pionair Apprentice Centre at Heathrow. It marked, as Nicholas put it, the end of 'nearly six years of ceaseless hope, faith and effort'.

Nicholas thanked everyone for the help they had so generously given – not only technically and financially but also by performing the myriad of unseen jobs like accounts and correspondence – and sprinkled Sigma's nose with champagne. With worries about the weather, the roll-out ceremony was conducted indoors, not for fear of what the wet might do to the Sigma's sleek new paintwork but out of respect for the assembled VIP guests, who would probably not enjoy rain running down their necks. The indoor ceremony also suited the men who had built the glider. They considered it appropriate that their creation was unveiled in the workshop, surrounded by the moulds, jigs and tools that had gone into its construction.

Popular Mechanics, an American magazine, reported on the Sigma in November 1972 – under the headline 'TRICK WING GLIDER GETS A LIFT WHEN IT NEEDS IT':

> 'Establishing proper wing area for a glider has always been a compromise. You need a broad wing for lift, a narrow one for speed. Go for one and you sacrifice the other.
>
> 'Now, a British aircraft expert, Rear Admiral Nicholas Goodhart, has come up with a variable-area wing that gives a glider a choice of lift or speed depending on thermal conditions. It has telescoping flaps at the trailing edges that slide in and out to vary the chord or width across the wing. Fully extended, the pneumatically controlled flaps increase wing area by 35 per cent.

'The variable wing enables a glider pilot to climb rapidly in a thermal with the flaps extended for maximum lift. Once aloft, he can retract the flaps for high speed sailing without the drag of a large wing. Speeds up to 165 mph are possible this way. With the flaps extended, the glider can soar lazily at speeds as low as 45 mph, making landings short and gentle. The sailplane has an overall wing span of just under 70 feet and a slim needle-nosed cockpit so shallow the pilot must control the ship from an almost prone position.

'The new design is currently being tested by Project Sigma, 47 Queen Ann St, London, England.'

The idea was that Sigma would make its maiden flight from Cranfield in August. The only question was who should have the honour of being the first pilot? All those sufficiently quali-fied tossed for the privilege of being at the controls for the first flight. The winner – perhaps inevitably – was Nicholas Goodhart and he was in the cockpit when, on 12th September 1971, Sigma at last took to the air.

By then Sigma was too late to compete in the 1970 World Championships in Texas, as originally intended. The target now was the event to be held in Yugoslavia in 1972 but unfor-tunately a serious drag problem – potentially cutting the glider's predicted performance by a crippling 50 per cent – was discovered, preventing Sigma from being entered in that competition either.

After conducting flight trials at Lasham in Hampshire, Nicholas believed that the problem might be due to imperfec-tions in the finish of the wing's leading edge or difficulties with the hinges on the flaps – or both – but he still had great faith in his creation.

'Assuming that the problems can be satisfactorily overcome, it is possible that Sigma could make its international competition debut in the next-but-one World Championships, which will take place in Australia in January 1974,' he reported.

But his confidence was misplaced. The problem of unwanted drag remained and no matter what the team tried, they could not overcome it. Eventually they were forced to admit, in an article in *Flight International* magazine in 1977, that they had hit an 'intractable problem'. Soon afterwards they accepted that they had no alternative but to admit defeat. They had almost achieved what they had set out to do but 'almost' wasn't enough.

There was no doubt that, despite all the problems, the Sigma concept worked and was a triumph in terms of aerodynamic efficiency. But the time taken to develop it, allied to the march of developments in general high performance glider design, meant that many of its advantages were overtaken by events.

As a report said at the time:

> 'The basic concept of large flaps giving an appreciable area and camber change has been shown to be practicable. The arrangement on this particular machine suffers from a number of defects – difficulties in adjusting the linkage, leaks, poor fairing – but there is no reason to suppose that they could not be eliminated by improvements to the detail design.'

The production team agreed with the US gliding magazine *Soaring* when it said it would be 'an unconscionable waste of first-rate research talent and considerable financial investment if Sigma were to fall by the wayside', so they advertised it as a free gift to 'any suitable applicant making proposals for further research'– tacitly admitting that the Sigma Project needed fresh thinking and, just as importantly, fresh financial backing.

The challenge was taken up by David Marsden, a professor of mechanical engineering at the University of Alberta in Canada, a record-breaking glider pilot who just happened to be on sabbatical at the time at the Cranfield Institute of Technology.

He moved Sigma to Canada in 1979 and made significant modifications, including the total replacement of the flap system, to establish it as a genuine contender in competition flying.

The Sigma – or an improved version of it, anyway – is still flying today, particularly in North America, and in 1997 broke the US 300 km triangle record by completing the course at an average of 157 kilometres per hour.

After the disappointment of the Sigma Project, Nicholas needed another challenge – and it wasn't long before he found it. Just as he had long dreamed of creating a glider that would lead the world, so too had he dreamed of building a flying machine powered only by human muscle.

It was British industrialist Henry Kremer who provided the impetus for this, Nicholas's next big venture. Kremer had lived in England since emigrating from his native Latvia after World War I and had become enormously successful as the inventor of wood products, particularly if they were connected to the burgeoning aviation industry (even in the era of aluminium, his special laminated plywoods, for example, were a key feature of the de Havilland Mosquito, nicknamed *The Wooden Wonder*).

It was his interest in flying, combined with his fascination with human fitness, that led to his offering the Kremer Prize – an initial £5,000, rising to £50,000 (a huge amount of money in those days) to anyone who could fly a human-powered aircraft around a mile-long figure-of-eight course.

By the mid-1970s the prize had still not been claimed, despite many attempts and, more importantly, Nicholas had time on his hands. To an aviation enthusiast, champion glider pilot, former test pilot, part-time inventor and recently retired senior naval officer it was too good an opportunity to resist.

With his knowledge of gliders, supported by all the experience he had gained from piloting almost 100 different types of powered aircraft, there was probably no one in the world with more of the necessary technical knowhow.

Not for the first time in his life, Nicholas had found the sort of challenge on which he thrived. He realised that one of the reasons all previous attempts had ended in failure was that the aircraft were simply too small. Any flying machine powered by nothing more than human muscles would have to be much bigger than any machine thus far designed for that purpose.

He resolved to build a truly huge aircraft with a 138-foot wingspan – as large as a Boeing 707 – using many of the principles employed by the gliders with which he was so familiar but with two fuselages, each containing a man on a bicycle.

There were two initial problems: firstly, finding somewhere with enough space to put his ideas into action and a runway wide enough to cope with the Manflyer's extraordinarily wide undercarriage and, secondly, recruiting at least two assistants young and fit enough to provide the muscle-power required to give the machine a chance of flying the required 10 feet above the ground.

Thanks to the esteem in which he was still held by his friends in the American forces, the first problem was easily overcome when he was quickly offered a spare hangar at Greenham Common, an air base near Newbury then being used by the US Air Force.

The second problem was almost as easily surmounted.

Simon Grant was an Oxford University student and qualified glider pilot who, because of his a long standing passion for flying, had written to Slingsby, the glider manufacturers, suggesting ways in which man-power might be used to help gliders fly further. Slingsby had politely declined interest, but while doing so mentioned that Nicholas Goodhart was looking for cyclists/pilots.

So Simon got in touch, cycled the 40 or so miles from Oxford to Nicholas's home in Inkpen a few times, proved he would be able to provide the necessary power output – and was taken on as one of the potential pilots. Simon was soon joined by Tony Wing, a London-based Army officer and helicopter pilot who, though a few years older, was just as fit thanks to his passion for long distance running. 'I agreed without fully realising the implications,' Tony admits.

For the next three years, from 1977 to 1980, the two men were key parts of the team which, working in Greenham Common's Hangar 301, put in 3,000 man-hours of effort developing the machine that Nicholas liked to call it his PBOP (Pedalled By Ordinary People) although it was officially known as the *Newbury Manflyer*.

They were not too surprised – or disheartened – when on 23rd August 1977 Nicholas's old American friend and fellow champion glider pilot Paul McCready won the first Kremer prize when his Gossamer Condor, piloted by Bryan Allen, achieved the first successful man-powered flight. There were, after all, other prizes still on offer – not least the £100,000 prize for the first man-powered machine to cross the English Channel.

Michael Moynihan reported on Nicholas's response to McCready's triumph in the *Sunday Times,* under the headline 'It May, Says The Admiral, Sound Like Pie In The Sky':

'For a moment or two, the world of Rear Admiral Nicholas Goodhart (Retd) crashed around him last week. For two years, he had worked on building a magnificent flying machine that would claim the coveted £50,000 prize for the world's first sustained man-powered flight.

Then, in California last Tuesday, an American pilot-cyclist beat him to it. Seated in the cockpit of his 70lb Gossamer Condor, with its 97ft wingspan, 24-year-old Bryan Allen pedalled energetically, activated a propeller connected to a bicycle chain and took off for a 1.4-mile flight on a figure of eight course.

But not for nothing did Goodhart, 57, think that he would be the first to accomplish man-powered flight. He knew his credentials were impeccable: ex-naval fighter pilot in the Second World War, inventor of the mirror deck landing system for aircraft carriers, designer of gliders and holder of the current United Kingdom gliding distance record of 360 miles.

Goodhart's hopes were pinned on his Newbury Manflyer which will be ready for a trial in a few weeks' time. It weighs 160lb, has a wing span of 137ft – the same as a Boeing 707 – and, to keep its two propellers working, two pilots will pedal away in modules 70ft apart.

Many people apart from Goodhart believe in his contraption. That's why all the materials that went into its construction, from balsa wood to aluminium, were supplied free by manufacturers.

But even before his Newbury Manflyer makes its trial flight, Goodhart is thinking ahead to his next – and most mind boggling – project. This is for the first man-powered flight across the English Channel. For this, he envisages adding a centre section to Newbury Manflyer, a module for a third pilot which would mean an extension of the wing of 210ft.

He believes that, cruising at about 17mph and about 10ft above the sea, the pedalling pilots could cover the 29-mile Dover-Calais trip in little more than one hour.

"It may sound like pie in the sky," Goodhart told me, "but there seems no logical reason why greater distances even than the Channel could not be achieved – depending largely, of course, on the stamina of the pilots. And there would be a positive advantage in flying over the sea as compared with land. There would not be the air disturbance you get when the sun warms up the earth.'"

Moynihan reported that Nicholas had suggested that, if a sponsor could be found to provide an attractive money prize, there would be many contenders if the Channel man-powered crossing attempt were turned into an international race – possibly starting in 1979 to mark the 70th anniversary of Bleriot's first flight across the Channel in an engine-powered aircraft.

But he said the Royal Aeronautical Society's man-powered aircraft group, which had been organising the contest for the £50,000 Kremer Prize had responded cautiously to Nicholas's idea. 'We are still at the teething stage of man-powered flight and it is early days to predict how it will progress,' Kenneth Clarke, the group's secretary, said.

The prospect of any man-powered aircraft being flown across the English Channel seemed a long way off to the people working with Nicholas Goodhart on the Manflyer project.

Indeed Tony Wing recalls that he was 'flabbergasted' when he saw what Nicholas was planning. Every other designer who had taken up the man-powered flight challenge was striving to design ever smaller, ever lighter machines – but here was a man insisting that the only answer was to build one with a wingspan every bit as wide as that of the world's biggest airliner. And it would be powered by two men on glorified bicycles! But he had no doubt that if anyone this side of the Atlantic was going to do it, it would probably be Nicholas Goodhart.

'He was totally focused on what we were doing – and maybe a bit distant because of it,' he recalls. 'He had conceived it, designed it and was building it. It was obvious that he saw it as his "baby".'

The Manflyer – an aircraft like no other – was described by one commentator at the time as 'one of the strangest aeroplanes in history'.

The pilots sat 70ft apart on their bicycle-like frames, which naturally had been specially designed for the purpose by Nicholas, and made of aluminium so light that each one weighed a mere 2lb. Each had just one control, a twist grip on the handlebars to control the elevator.

There were no ailerons, no rudder and no brakes or any kind – if they needed to stop, they either stopped pedalling or, if something rather more drastic was required, reached a leg forward and pressed a shoe against the front wheel.

To yaw, right or left, one pilot simply had to pedal harder than the other; to roll, one applied up-elevator while the other didn't; and to pitch both pilots did. Tony, on the right hand side bicycle, was given the job of looking after height and airspeed; Simon, on the left, was in charge of roll and yaw.

The machine was made of plastic heat-shrunk over extraordinarily light expanded polystyrene and balsa wood formers, stretched over a frame of plywood main spar and spruce booms and driven forward by propellers on pylons, connected to each bicycle by chains.

One of the potential problems was how the two pilots were doing to get into the transparent cocoons which were their cockpits – such fripperies as doors and traditional access methods were ruled out because of their weight. This was overcome by Simon who, on one of his visits to Nicholas's house and workshop, designed a simple frame which he and Tony could use to clamber inside.

'I was really chuffed about that,' Simon says. 'To have someone like Nicholas accepting my design for something – who'd have thought it?'

Many people apart from Goodhart believed in the Manflyer, which is why all the materials needed for its construction had been donated – free – by industry.

Some of the plane's construction work was tackled by Nicholas's friends and relatives, but most was eventually done by members of the Newbury & District Model Aircraft Society, whose help Nicholas had enlisted with the promise that he would give them each £1 from the eventual prize for every hour (properly recorded, of course) that they spent on the project.

But while the model aircraft enthusiasts had been able to do their construction work in the evening or at weekends, the two pilots had to be available at rather less sociable times of the day.

They had no idea whether or when Nicholas would be requiring their services until he telephoned them – after a late-night check of the next day's weather forecast – just a few hours before he wanted them at Greenham Common.

'He would look at the forecast at 11 o'clock or midnight,' says Tony, 'and tell us we had to be there by six. For me, working in London and living on the South Coast, it was quite difficult! And even then it would be a wasted journey if the wind had happened to get up overnight.'

The wind was a constant problem. A flying machine so big had to be dragged out of the hangar sideways, on trolleys, before being manhandled to the runway. Any undue wind – or even a gentle breeze coming from the wrong direction – was enough to put the whole project on hold. As Nicholas said at the time:

> 'The wind is the biggest problem we have had throughout. The machine is so light it would blow away if the wind was any stronger than two kilometres per hour.'

The team discovered that there were only around six days a year when conditions were right for flying – unlike in America, where Paul McCready was enjoying being able to fly his man-powered machine almost whenever he wanted to.

'We are very jealous of the Americans,' Nick said, as yet another potential flying day was ruined by a vigorous breeze.

In the early days when flying did seem possible, the two pilots climbed onto their bicycles while Nicholas climbed into his car, stuck his head out of the sunroof and bellowed instructions at them through a megaphone as his wife Molly drove him in their faithful Citroen down the runway.

Later on even he agreed this was not strictly necessary and as work progressed it became clear that what worked best was for each pilot to look after himself and let the other one do the same.

Although the Manflyer had not yet taken to the air, Nicholas was already working out how it would be able to claim the next Kremer prize by flying across the English Channel. He reckoned that if he extended the wingspan to 210ft it would be big enough to house a bicycle for a third pilot, who would be necessary to provide enough power to keep the machine airborne for the hour it would take to cover the 29 miles from Dover to Calais.

Tony Wing, for one, was not so enthusiastic. He knew that the Manflyer needed an unusually long and wide runway – and that there was no such thing anywhere near Dover.

'I had visions of us being pushed off Beachy Head or something – that was the only way I could see the Manflyer ever being launched with enough height for a flight like that,' he says. 'Once in the air we might have been able to build up enough power to keep it flying, but I doubt it. It doesn't bear thinking about, to be honest!'

Such considerations were made academic in June 1979 when Paul MacCready's Gossamer Albatross – again piloted by Bryan Allen – managed to win Henry Kremer's £100,000 prize by flying across the Channel from England to France.

Nicholas and his team were disappointed but not deterred. He described the Americans' achievement as 'super – absolutely first class' – then set out to prove that his invention was just as good, if not better. He had come too far to give up now. After a career that had seen so much technical achievement, it had become a matter of pride for him to see if his design would work.

Fortunately, most of his team agreed with him and, by the end of that year, they were ready to try to put their own creation into the air. On a trial run down the runway, just to see if the two pilots could steer the machine in a straight line, Nicholas proclaimed: 'It taxied well and nothing broke. All very satisfying.'

But, as so often with matters aeronautic, the weather intervened and it was several weeks before conditions were good enough to put the Manflyer through its paces as a machine that might actually fly.

But on 1st January 1980 – a beautiful, still and crisp morning just made for flying – the Newbury Manflyer at last got off the frost-covered ground. Twice.

'I remember the wing coming up between the cockpits, just as one would expect – very gracefully – and suddenly realising I wasn't on the ground any more,' Simon, who by then was a teacher in Oxford and about to get married, recalls. 'It didn't feel particularly strenuous. In fact I felt I could have kept it up for quite some time.'

On its first flight the Manflyer took off at about 16mph and flew 3ft above the ground for a promising 400 yards in precisely 69 seconds.

'I feel absolutely delighted,' Nicholas told a watching BBC TV crew. 'We have demonstrated that two chaps can fly this sort of man-powered aeroplane – and that's what our four years' work was for, as far as I am concerned.'

The team's euphoria did not last long, however, for on the second attempt the Manflyer suffered some damage to a wing spar which rendered it unable to fly again for three months.

Nicholas was not too downhearted. He had, to some extent at least, proved his point. And anyway, he said, the snapped spar was probably 'just one of those things'.

'The reason it broke was not because the design was wrong,' he said. 'It was because we made a slight mistake in putting together and some of the glue got left out. All we have to do is put it back the same and I am reasonably confident it will then be strong enough.'

With hindsight, Tony Wing believes the broken spar was a blessing in disguise.

'I have a feeling we would probably have wrecked the thing,' he says. 'I had a fear that one pilot would overpower the other one, and if that had happened after we were airborne we would have been in trouble, because once we had left the runway we would have had to do a complete 360-degree turn to land on it again – and we would never have managed that.'

The team never found out if Tony's fears were well founded, for before the machine could fly again, the USAF effectively put an end to the Manflyer experiment. The Americans told Nicholas he would have to leave because there would be no room for them any more. The airbase was about to become the most closely guarded, most secret military installation in Britain. It was being expanded to become the home of 96 Cruise nuclear missiles.

So it was that, rather than being known as the place where two men on bikes came to fly, Greenham Common went down in history for something else altogether.

On 5th September 1981, a group of Welsh women marched from Cardiff to Greenham and delivered to the base commander a letter which, among other things, stated: 'We fear for the future of all our children and for the future of the living world which is the basis of all life'.

When their request for a debate was ignored they set up a Peace Camp just outside the perimeter fence – and stayed there, supported by thousands of women from all over the world, for nearly 20 years as the focus of a campaign that threw a spotlight on nuclear weapons.

The Manflyer, meanwhile, was taken apart, packed up and moved to Wroughton RAF base, near Swindon, where there was no runway wide enough for it to fly.

Nicholas was still vaguely optimistic that his Manflyer might one day fly again. 'There is always the possibility that somebody may in due course push it out again and have another go,' he said.

He eventually hoisted his creation into the roof of the Wroughton science museum, where it stayed, held by an elaborate system of ropes and pulleys, until someone started a hovercraft beneath it and it fell to the floor, shattering into a million pieces.

Nicholas, a man who rarely allowed his emotions to show, said simply that he was 'devastated'.

Nobody who knew Nicholas would have expected the demise of the Manflyer to be his final attempt at a high-profile invention. Just as he had found other ideas to occupy his time and, more importantly, his brain, after his retirement from the Navy, the end of his gliding career, the failure of the Sigma project... so now was he able to turn his attention to something else.

If ever there was a man who believed that when one door closes another opens, it was Nicholas Goodhart – and the door that opened at this relatively late stage of his life led to an aeroplane with a wingspan of an incredible three kilometres!

Nicholas, like some of the world's top scientific brains at the time, had long been trying to work out a way of preventing the sort of hurricanes which all too often caused dreadful havoc and loss of life, particularly along the eastern coast of the American continents. He reckoned that even if you ignored the terrible human death toll (which on its own was too high a price to pay), the huge financial costs of natural disasters merited some serious research into ways of preventing them.

With characteristic Goodhart thoroughness, Nicholas calculated that each hurricane cost around 80 billion dollars and, with up to ten major hurricanes expected in the North Atlantic and Eastern Pacific zones in any one year, the cost to mankind was enormous.

No wonder some of the world's most imaginative engineers, inventors and scientists – Microsoft boss Bill Gates among them – had spent years trying to find ways of preventing them. And no wonder it became the major project which occupied so much of Nicholas Goodhart's time in the final years of his life.

Nicholas was in his mid-80s by the time he began to turn the thoughts inside his head into something more tangible – his

Albedo Hurricane Buster. He started from the premise that hurricanes begin as relatively light winds and it is only energy from the sun that – by evaporating water from the surface of the sea – turns those breezes into the terrifying destructive force that is the full-blown hurricane.

If that is what causes hurricanes, he reasoned, *the solution must be to find a way of stopping such evaporation.* It made sense to prevent solar energy from causing the conditions that turned a weak airflow system into something stronger.

In a press release issued at the start of the project, Nicholas admitted: 'Tackling the forces of nature is not to be undertaken lightly'.

But that did not mean he would not try! Nicholas's solution was typically cutting edge – effectively to drop a lid on any embryo hurricanes as they formed in the ocean, to put a barrier between the sun and the sea. His proposed means of doing this was a huge flying boat, which would land on the sea and cover the water with an enormous sheet of polymer (similar to the material used for packets of potato crisps), which would reflect some of the incoming solar radiation back into space, thus removing enough power from the area to interfere with the hurricane formation process.

Nicholas's flying boats would have a wingspan at least 30 times greater than any that had been built before. After landing on the sea, the huge machine would lay out 25 square kilometres of reflective material behind it – and collect it all up again when the job was done.

The thought of designing such a huge flying machine did not dismay Nicholas in the slightest. It would be created by joining together a series of 99 identical flying boats, each with a wingspan of a mere 30 metres, then fixing a one-winged unit on each side.

When he learned that about 100 square kilometres of sea would have to be covered in reflective material for the system to work, his solution was equally simple: use four such giant aircraft side by side.

The fact that each Albedo system – with the reflective sheets disgorged from four aircraft covering a total of 100 square kilometres of ocean – would require a total of 396 units and eight wing tip units did not deter him either. It made the whole project more practicable. As he said at the time, 'The multiplicity of similar units required enables mass production techniques to be used from the start, thus greatly reducing the total cost.'

The monster machine would be propelled by possibly as many as 101 turbo-prop engines, evenly distributed across the span on pylons above the wing and, as if a plane with a 3 km wingspan was not big enough, Nicholas was already considering building something even bigger.

'There is no structural reason for the span to be limited to 3 kilometres,' he said.

No structural reason, maybe, but flying an even bigger version might be a problem, as even Nicholas admitted. Since the aircraft would have to make a series of 180-degree turns – both in the air and on the water – a 3km wingspan was about as big as would be practicable, he realised. Even then, to turn such a huge machine would take about 5½ minutes and 'any longer times than this are considered excessive', he said.

Nicholas was convinced the Albedo system would work; it was just a question of who would be willing to provide the funds to make it happen. After five years' research he reported:

'The scale of this invention cannot be underestimated and is likely to attract considerable attention around the world. It is now ready for development and is seeking investment. The

Albedo project is likely to appeal to US Government agencies and the governments in other major countries affected by hurricanes and also to major scientific or engineering companies interested in the development and construction of the system.'

With hurricanes and their devastating destructive powers being so newsworthy, Nicholas's Albedo solution captured media attention – not least in the *Western Morning News*, which gave it a full page feature in which writer Graeme Demianyk described 'an imaginative system to reflect solar radiation back into space by using plastic sheets akin to crisp packets'.

Demianyk wrote:

'The plan is to remove the destructive power of hurricanes by deploying seaplanes to drag five-mile strips of reflective plastic across the sea. Since it is the ocean's warm surface that gives a hurricane its destructive power, Rear Admiral Goodhart's system relies on preventing the warming process by bouncing sunshine back into the atmosphere. He believes his Albedo device – named after the scientific measurement of reflectivity – can massively reduce lives lost and billion dollar costs. Hurricane Katrina killed 2,000 people and cost more than 81 billion dollars.

'The Admiral reckons that previous remedies, chiefly those that have fallen out of the US equivalent of the Met Office, have failed because they approached the problem from the wrong direction.'

Demianyk reported that Nicholas had explained his idea thus: 'All the others tried to fix hurricanes. That's ludicrous. They are far too powerful. I just try to stop them starting.'

After describing the Albedo system in detail, Demianyak's article went on:

'Naturally, he is prepared for people to question the engineering and science, acknowledging that on first inspection the plan appears to be 'beyond the bounds of feasibility.'

'But,' the writer pointed out, 'there had also been reservations about Goodhart's hugely successful mirror deck landing system.'

Nicholas had told the *Western Morning News*:

'Everyone is sceptical to begin with. I expect everyone to be sceptical about this one, which is why I've developed a complete proposal which deals with all the things they are going to dream up in order to say it's impossible. I can tell them: "Well, I've thought of that".'

Nicholas told Demianyk that the Met Office in Exeter was ambivalent: 'They said, "Well, we don't have hurricanes, so goodbye." If they had adopted it, they could have got Britain ahead of everybody. Now I'm going to go to an American.'

The Albedo project was an exciting prospect and one that could ultimately save many more lives than the few hundred saved by Nicholas's most successful invention, the mirror deck landing system. However, it was not to be...

One of Nicholas's acquaintances in the Met Office came up with the news that the theory upon which he had based the Hurricane Buster was flawed. It turned out that the driving force for hurricanes was not, as he had believed, directly linked to evaporation caused by the sun shining on the sea, but was more to do with random waves of barometric pressure passing over ocean surface water that had been warmed up by the sun.

A subtle difference, perhaps – and maybe one fully appreciated only by experts in meteorology – but it was enough to bring the Hurricane Buster to a halt and, in July 2010, Nicholas reported to his supporters:

'To all those who have so freely given their time in helping me with my Albedo (hurricane buster) invention I write sadly to tell you that the project is now dead in the water. It has been torpedoed in the engine room by a research scientist at the Met Office.'

But Nicholas, even at the age of 91, was not disheartened. Yet again – as had happened so often throughout his life – as one door was closing another was opening.

'However, all is not lost,' he reported. 'There are other applications of the invention to which its special characteristics could bring huge benefit.'

The Albedo – which seemed to have come so close to eradicating hurricanes – could easily be adapted to be used even more effectively for fighting forest fires.

'At least, that is what I envisage at present,' he said confidently. 'But there is much to be explored before I can harden up the proposal.

His idea was that an aircraft (with a wingspan of 500 metres rather than the Hurricane Buster's 3 kilometres) would scoop up maybe 500 tonnes of water from the sea, then fly along the fire line using thermal detectors to control which of the many nozzles across the span needed to be open at any time in order to blanket the hottest parts of the fire. On board air compressors would provide the air supply to enable the modern technique of putting down a cloud of atomised water sufficient to deny the oxygen necessary for combustion. The system would only work within about 60 miles of the ocean, he admitted, but since that is where most forest fires occur that would not be too much of a problem.

And that was not the only potential use for his invention.

It could also be used for the speedy provision of international aid to areas struck by major natural disasters, in particular where the local infrastructure (airports, roads and seaports) had been destroyed.

Or it could be used to carry general freight.

Or (if the aircraft were fitted with huge wheels and low pressure tyres) it could be used to transport agricultural freight to and from areas of wide open grassland without traditional airports.

The future for Nicholas's great invention appeared, to him anyway, exciting and unlimited.

And it is probably appropriate that it was still taking up much of his time, thought and energy when, on 9th April 2011, he died.

He was 91 and had achieved more than most of us could ever dream of.

10. Goodhart – the man they knew

WITH UNDERSTATEMENT of which her beloved husband would have approved, Molly Goodhart describes Nicholas as, 'an unusual man'. Brilliant, brave, complex, cussed, curt, cold, introverted, irascible – people who knew him, but not well, employed a veritable lexicon of adjectives to describe his character, about which there was frequently contradictory judgment.

As Nicholas made his way through the ranks of the Royal Navy, one assessment from a senior officer described his personality as 'angular' (i.e. sharp or awkward in manner) and 'lacking in tact'. Another referred to his 'cynicism'; one more to his 'lack of patience with civilians'. But in the same personal files are appraisals which noted his pleasantness, his sense of humour and his popularity with all ranks.

Readers of those files might conclude that the word *enigmatic* could well have been invented to describe Nicholas Goodhart.

The shyness of his childhood never fully left him, nor did the adherence to the Victorian values of his upbringing – the stiff upper lip, the shunning of any public display of emotion or affection, the rigid application at all times of good manners and the proper and precise use of the English language.

But those close to him saw through that veneer and into the heart of a warm, loving, kind, generous and humorous man.

'He was,' says Molly, with deep sincerity and conviction, 'the love of my life'.

It was a love that for years remained platonically confined by a code of moral conduct so strict that it is today beyond comprehension but at its time was unbreakable without incurring much cruel condemnation.

Nicholas was Molly's husband's boss in the Fleet Air Arm in the early 1950s and for many years she and Nicholas kept to themselves the love they felt for each other while, as literally 'just good friends', often confiding in each other. That shared confidence allowed Nicholas to talk often to Molly about his unhappy marriage to his American first wife, whom he had met in 1953 when his Naval career took him to Washington. Nicholas was then in his early thirties but his shyness and dedication to his career and his sport had combined to ensure that, until then, he had never had a steady girlfriend. When, in 1957, she told him she was pregnant, Nicholas did the honourable thing and in 1958 he married her. They never had a child – the baby was lost, it was said – and they were, says Molly, "locked in an unhappy marriage" until the early 1970s, when Nicholas and Molly finally and publicly became 'an item' and set up home together.

It wasn't until 1975 that Nicholas finally got the divorce he wanted and married Molly. He was 56; Molly was 47. Thus, much later in life than most, Nicholas and Molly began a devoted marriage and Nicholas became stepfather to Molly's three children, Alyson, Ian and Fiona Corner.

This was a huge change to the life of Nicholas Goodhart. Childless in his 56 years, more than a decade of which had been in that unhappy marriage, this solitary, private, shy and reserved man, comfortable in his own company, tending towards insularity in his lifestyle and demeanour, suddenly had to adapt to bustling family life. Molly recalls: 'It was so different to the life he'd been accustomed to and I often asked him "Are you happy?" He would reply "Yes, darling. I really am. Very happy".'

And their marriage was to endure in that happiness for nearly 40 years.

After the pain of his first marriage, Nicholas had in Molly not just his first and only real love but a true soul mate; someone, perhaps the *only* one, who could fathom and cope with his complex character.

For example, Molly understood and rationalised Nicholas's inability ever to engage in outward displays of affection towards her.

'This didn't bother me at all,' she says. 'I knew that it was just the way he was, one of the consequences of his upbringing. He would never kiss me or even hold my hand in public. For instance, at New Year's Eve parties when all the couples kissed each other to welcome in the New Year, Nicholas wouldn't kiss me – not until we got home. Then he would give me a kiss and say: "Happy New Year, my darling." When we were out walking, he would never take hold of my hand but sometimes I would hold *his* hand and I sensed that he liked that, even though he would not show it.'

They had many shared interests. Molly learned to fly gliders – a rare accomplishment for a woman in those days – and she enjoyed the genuine respect of men as an equal in male dominated environments; an equality earned long before it became politically correct and consequently demanded.

Says Molly's son Ian: 'He loved Molly very much and she him in equal measure. Molly provided Nick with the home, the love, the family, the laughter, the wonderful cuisine, together with an ability to orchestrate a damned good party for two to two hundred with ease – amongst but a few of her many skills and accomplishments. He, in turn, was her rock, her 'man', as she described him on his deathbed as he breathed his last. They were undoubtedly a damned good team together – chalk and cheese as well as the perfect couple where two halves make a complete whole.'

Having set up home at Inkpen, Nicholas and Molly shared a love of canal boating. They owned a small craft, *Heron*, on the Kennet and Avon canal and took charge of grounds maintenance and stewardship of the first downstream lock from Kintbury.

Says Ian: 'We often took a picnic and a mower and in between jobs we waved at the commuters with Railway Children-esque enthusiasm before chugging home to moor up near the Dundas Arms.'

In the summer of 1982, an event on the canal, organised by Nicholas and Molly, was reported in the local newspaper, the *Newbury Weekly News*, thus:

> 'For three hours on Saturday afternoon the Kennet long boat became the Admiral's barge as Nicholas and Molly Goodhart entertained a party of guests from London.
>
> 'Rear Admiral Goodhart, from Inkpen, has for the past twelve months held office as Master of the City Guild of Grocers and it was his wish to thank all the employees of Grocers' Hall who had served him well during his year of office.
>
> 'A coach was organised to bring the Beadle and the Clerk, the kitchen, serving and administrative staff with their wives and husbands from the City to Newbury Wharf where the Admiral and Mrs Goodhart and Polly the dog welcomed them aboard.
>
> 'The barge cast off, the wine began to flow and the visitors from London relaxed, enjoying the perfect weather, the Berkshire countryside and the delicious array of appetising dishes

which had been planned, cooked and assembled by Mrs Goodhart herself.

'While the barge turned round many passengers went ashore, some to paddle and soak up the sun. The boat arrived back at the Wharf and the merry company disembarked to climb aboard their waiting coach for the journey back to the city.'

Nicholas and Molly frequently barged in France and relied on each other, with deft teamwork, as skipper and crew. In similar fashion over many years they toured Europe in camper vans, enjoying the simple good life and beauty the Continent had to offer, way off the beaten tourist track.

They shared a love of good cuisine, both being accomplished cooks, and meals prepared by Nicholas were invariably produced with military precision and served promptly to the very minute of his strictly pre-determined time. Lunch at 12.30 meant lunch at 12.30. Exactly.

'He cooked excellent meals,' Molly will tell you – but it was an attribute for which Nicholas sought no acclaim.

'Anybody who can read can cook,' he would say.

Not that he was a bookworm – the very opposite, in fact. He never read a novel in his life. He had no time for them at all.

'It's just somebody else's imagination,' he would say.

He would read technical books, when he had to, but invariably lost patience before he had finished them.

Nicholas was very knowledgeable about wine. He loved fine wine and port and took great pride and pleasure in introducing close friends and family to the wonderful wines from the Grocers Company cellar – a genuine privilege for those fortunate enough to be chosen for it. At home, Nicholas regarded his daily glass of Madeira, then wine at lunch, as an 'absolute must'.

Happy though they were at Inkpen, Nicholas and Molly loved the West Country and cherished a shared dream of buying a house on an estuary where he could build a steam engine and they could both go spinning for mackerel. That ambition had to be put on hold, however, because Nicholas had professional interests which necessitated living within commuting distance of London.

He had retired from the Royal Navy as a Rear Admiral in 1973 but rapidly built a very busy post retirement career. For seven years he was a consultant to the Boeing Aircraft Company, looking after their military interests in London and being particularly concerned with the sale of HMS *Speedy*, a hydrofoil vessel, to the Royal Navy and of the Chinook helicopter to the Royal Air Force.

In 1981-82 he was the Master of the Worshipful Company of Grocers in the City of London and from 1982 he held various company directorships, including non-executive Chairman of the Lancashire & Yorkshire Assurance Society.

In 1977 he joined Lloyd's of London – the global insurance market based in the City; he became increasingly involved with Lloyd's and, right up until his death in 2011, operated as a private limited company.

Edward Vale, at the Association of Lloyd's Members, explains:

> 'Nicholas Goodhart was an external member of Lloyd's of London. He had joined as a 'Name' in 1977. While his initial years may have been relatively uneventful and profitable, the arrival of huge losses across the London-based marketplace in the early 1990s meant that much of the middle period of his membership was the polar opposite.
>
> 'He had joined the Association of Lloyd's Members soon after its formation in 1982. It had been set up by Names to represent

them and to provide them with better information about Lloyd's and its syndicates, as well as about the members and managing agents active in the market.

'Nicholas became a regular and interested participant in the Association's conferences both in London and the West Country and few took place at which he did not ask the speakers a number of penetrating questions. Later, he became founder member of an informal group of Names based in the south-west which met a few times each year to discuss Lloyd's issues, often in the company of an invited underwriter or members' agent.

'During the late 1990s Lloyd's was changing rapidly. It initiated a form of risk-based capital provision, attempting to match more accurately the amount of capital put up by members to back underwriting premium. Names participated on a number of different syndicates and classes of business, such as aviation, motor and marine as well as property and reinsurance.

'Lloyd's used a complex calculation to assess capital but Nicholas believed that, while right in principle, this provided neither sufficient credit for a Name's diversification nor sufficient penalties to a corporate member, most of whom backed just one syndicate run by its parent company. Undaunted (of course!) by his status as an outsider, nor by the machinations of the City and Lloyd's, he visited the Lloyd's team of mathematical boffins on a number of occasions and persuaded them to provide him with the detail from which they produced their capital requirement.

'Then, working at home on his computer and producing numerous complex spreadsheets, Nicholas was able to convince Lloyd's that a spread of insurance business, such as underwritten by nearly all Names, merited a discount from the base calculation.

'Although members' agents and the Association of Lloyd's Members itself were also actively trying to make the system fairer to Names, it was generally accepted by them that his role as a Name rather than an "insider", allied to the intellectual strength of his arguments, was critical in persuading Lloyd's to adjust its methodology.

'This produced a gradual increase in the differentiation of capital required between members who supported only one syndicate versus those whose collateral was spread across many. In 2001, both types of member had an average capital to under-writing ratio of 48%. By 2009, Names' capital requirement averaged 39%, while so-called "dedicated" members provided 61% capital in support of their single syndicate.

'His campaign of dogged determination was a singular success, one of which Nicholas – but also, perhaps, the new Lloyd's – could be proud.

'Nicholas made many friends associated with Lloyd's during his time as a Name. He was both interested in and interested about his financial venture, despite it being so different to his military career. Other facets of his life show this same breadth of intellect and his astonishing energy, well into his eighties, was typical of a truly remarkable man.'

The South West Lloyd's Discussion Group, to which Edward Vale refers, was formed by Nicholas Goodhart and Commander Robin Leighton and has now been going for at least 25 years. Its chairman, Lord Wynford of Wynford Eagle, Dorset says:

'As far as I am aware, this Group is unique in Britain and we currently have 15 members drawn from Devon, Dorset and Somerset. We have six monthly meetings to which we invite knowledgeable and influential speakers down from London and we can cover an enormous amount of business.'

Lord Wynford describes Nicholas Goodhart as having been 'a very intelligent' member of the Group:

'His particular interest was the Lloyd's system of Risk Based Capital under which all of us underwrite in the Market and we could be sure that if he was going to present one of his complex but logical arguments to the Group we would need our ice-packed towels wound tightly around our heads if we were to have any chance of understanding what he was going on about!

'He was a lovely, charming man who we all miss.'

The time and energy Nicholas devoted to Lloyd's and to the Company of Grocers were so formidable that they would have done more than justice to a man half his age.

He loved the Company of Grocers, to which his lengthy period of involvement (and particularly his stewardship as Master) was both a consuming duty and a highly pleasurable pursuit. Similarly, his dedication to Lloyd's and his supreme professionalism in its business moved Michael Deeny, former Chairman of the Association of Lloyd's Members, to write:

> 'Admiral Goodhart was a man of wide ranging energy and intellectual abilities and a name at Lloyd's. It was typical of his courage and judgment that he continued underwriting after his heavy losses of the 1990s. His mathematical abilities enabled him to make a vital contribution to decisions on capital requirements in the new, more risk conscious Lloyd's.'

However, in 1987 Nicholas and Molly resolved that they could, at last, fulfil that dream of a move to the West Country. They bought Church House, a rambling old rectory at Uffculme in Devon.

They loved their life at the old rectory, where they were able to indulge their desire for the rural idyll, even if their attempts at self-sufficiency were not always successful – such as when they bought a pair of geese to fatten up for the Christmas festivities. Come the time, they simply could not bring themselves to 'complete the process', so the geese – who they called 'Sage' and 'Onion' – became much-loved family pets instead. And so they remained until a fox intervened, separating Onion from her head and leaving Sage deeply despondent until the acquisition of a new partner proved just how fickle even seemingly devoted ganders can be!

Nicholas never did build his steam engine but he did achieve the next best thing – driving the Dart Valley steam train from Totnes, an adventure from which, according to Molly, he came home like an excited little boy.

He and Molly both loved train journeys, on which he would always talk to the drivers, and even the excitement of the Dart Valley experience was exceeded the day he spent almost the whole journey in the cab of a diesel engine and persuaded the driver to let him take the controls from Barrow-in-Furness to Crewe.

Renowned journalist, broadcaster and Guardian columnist Simon Hoggart, husband of Nicholas's stepdaughter Alyson, recalled a railway journey with him from Newton Abbot to Paddington '...during which Nick was able to account for every variation in the train's speed. "Ah, the Hungerford gradient," he would say, or "That's the Didcot interchange...".'

Eventually, Nicholas and Molly concluded that the old rectory had become too big and, with typically adventurous spirit, they moved, in 1995, to become the first residents of an exciting new development.

Lindridge Park is 23 acres of beautiful South Devon countryside in which, until it was completely destroyed by a ferocious fire in 1963, stood historic Lindridge House, one of England's most stunning stately homes. In the early 1990s emerged a plan to turn Lindridge Park into an exclusive, very private and highly prestigious estate of 21 luxury homes. In addition to the breathtaking houses, the development included fully restored Grade One listed gardens, paddocks, swimming pool and tennis courts.

It was a brave, challenging, innovative concept and as such tailor-made for a certain retired Rear Admiral and his equally adventurous wife. The Goodharts became the pioneering occupants. Ian takes up the story:

> 'They were the first Lindridge occupants to arrive in what has now filled to the 21 planned homes on an Italianate garden of incredible beauty. They have both contributed across the piece. Nick was gardener, before the contract was finalised, and swimming pool monitor, too. For several years he was the highest ranked non-stipended pool cleaner in the West! He was also Chair of the Residents Association, a role in which his military skills often subdued the odd dissenter or troublemaker. I recall him gently owning up to the fact that handling one or two of them was more demanding than any task in the MoD.
>
> 'He took charge of the plumbing and waterworks on the estate for many years and if you can imagine a scene similar to a roadside telecommunications junction box being serviced, with wires everywhere, this engineer knew every pipe, every water pressure, every valve and every "action on" should anything go wrong in any of the miles of waterways and tributes, sinkholes and gullies throughout the Lindridge Estate. That was his way. Attention to detail, accurate, precise, logical and (sometimes infuriatingly) always right, too. Amongst many others, I'm sure, I grew in time to appreciate, respect, rely upon and revere those qualities.'

And so the epilogue of the truly remarkable life of Nicholas Goodhart was to be played out in what became the tranquil beauty of Lindridge. He settled in that lovely home with Molly and savoured every minute of the time they had left together.

'There was a bond,' says Molly, 'a true bond. Often we would sit together in silence, very peaceably, but I always knew what he was thinking. At other times, we would laugh a lot. We had such a lot of fun.'

Nicholas rarely watched television, never watched a video or visited a cinema, never owned a camera or a mobile phone. But he loved maps and would consult them earnestly, planning routes for the journeys he made with Molly. He always had a good car, his last being a state-of-the-art eco-friendly electric hybrid, which he would proudly demonstrate.

He was a great fan of genealogy and wrote, with typically meticulous attention to detail, the Goodhart Family Tree. And he worked, of course, on his ceaseless inventions – stopping only to raid the handy drawer in his desk, which he kept stocked full of his favourite dark chocolate, courtesy of his seven grandchildren, who always knew what to give him for birthdays and Christmas.

His computer was an essential component of his everyday life, though his affection for it was not shared by Molly, to whom it was 'that festering machine'! On his computer he would document, calculate, register and record whatever projects he had currently in hand and he never lost his love of engineering.

When not engaged in all that, he would be solving Sudoku puzzles, getting stuck into a bit of DIY or consulting the dictionary before announcing the correct definition of impossibly difficult words.

Until, towards his end, it became impossible, he also walked miles every day – timing each walk exactly with stopwatch, pedometer and calorific calculator before analysing the benefits, so as to announce to Molly (and her chagrin!) the exact subsequent consumption allowance. Although intensely irritated by the increasing immobility of his latter days, he came to regard his stair-lift as a friend – an essential gadget in ensuring that he didn't spill a drop of his gin and tonic in transit.

Nicholas hardly ever showed emotion but there was one very notable and significant occasion upon which he did.

Molly was looking to 'de-clutter' some of her possessions, among them a collection of real fur teddy bears.

'Such a shame to throw these out,' she thought. So she resolved to give them to Children's Hospice South West instead. Nicholas accompanied her to hand over the bears to the Little Bridge House Children's Hospice, near Barnstaple in North Devon. They were given a tour of the premises and, as they played with the children, Molly saw a man she'd never seen before. As they left, Nicholas's eyes were full of tears.

The hospice became his favourite charity and he made local front page and TV news when, to raise funds for it, he abseiled down the 120ft tower of Cullompton Parish Church – a considerable feat for a young man – at the age of 88!

Nicholas's support for Children's Hospice South West is hugely appreciated by the charity, where co-founder and chief executive Eddie Farwell recalls:

> 'From the very first time Nicholas visited Little Bridge House, our children's hospice in North Devon, the life-limited children and families that stay with us captured his heart and this is where our fond relationship with Nicholas and Molly began.
>
> 'Nicholas made significant personal donations to Children's Hospice South West and in addition, he gave his personal backing to a funding bid to The Worshipful Company of Grocers in London. That resulted in a grant of £30,000 towards our new hospice, Little Harbour, in Cornwall. We are so very lucky that Nicholas was able to help us forge that link and we are convinced that this would not have been achieved without him.
>
> 'Nicholas was a highly intelligent man with a fascinating life story and his achievements throughout that life were nothing short of remarkable. What a true inspiration he was and will

always be to so many and we were extremely grateful to be the recipient of his kindness, support and generosity.'

Kindness, support and generosity, almost the same words as those used by Lance Cole – now a successful writer, particularly on aviation – who was lucky enough to grow up in Inkpen while Nicholas Goodhart was living there. He recalls a kind and clever man who always made time to talk to him and give advice.

'I met Rear Admiral Goodhart, a near neighbour at Inkpen, when I was a teenager. He kindly took me to see his Newbury Manflier project and its Greenham trials and I was honoured to help him move it to the Science Museum store. I also went out on his motor boat, which was great fun. Imagine being captained on the Kennet and Avon Canal by a Rear Admiral!

'I could never call him "Nicholas", he was always "Admiral" or "Sir". In later years, we would travel up to London on the train together from Kintbury and he always looked at my design work and photography. He took time to encourage me and offer firm advice. Years later, after a long gap in contact, I asked him for help with my biography of his old colleague and friend Beverley Shenstone – the man who shaped the Spitfire's wing and went on to design gliders. Shenstone had worked with Goodhart on the design of the Sigma glider. Once again, Nicholas took the time to help me.

'To me, Nicholas Goodhart was a man to be respected, an old-school Naval officer who I showed due deference to. He may have had a tough ex- Dartmouth/Royal Navy shell, but underneath he quietly helped young people such as myself.

'I think that very few people knew how many of us he helped and encouraged. Such kindness made its mark and was a lesson to me and others. He was a talented engineer/inventor and sadly, our society is rapidly being denuded of such remarkable people. We don't seem to make people like H.C.N. Goodhart anymore, and it is our loss. I am truly privileged to have met him.'

Nicholas Goodhart died on 9th April 2011, following a massive stroke, at the age of 91. At a London Memorial Service in his honour, his stepson Ian captured this exceptional man's unique character in a moving eulogy, which ended thus:

'Nicholas was unhurried, unflappable, knowledgeable, generous, detailed, precise and kindly. He always gave sound and measured advice to all. He had an endearing and enduring smile which beamed as a welcome to guests both informally at home and at corporate and civic events whenever he greeted others.

'He loved and lived life to the full. He rose to various heights in many ways, achieved and accomplished much on national and international stages in aviation and invention, service to the Grocers Company and to the Lloyd's financial institution, always with modesty and charm.

'He died in a dignified, peaceful and mercifully swift and painless way. His memory will endure in so many different ways in all our hearts and his love and care for Molly will bring her continued pride and treasured memories of their long and joyful time together.

'Let us now join together uplifted in spirit and admiration in celebration of Nicholas's amazing innings; and as we each say our fond farewells in our own way with a tribute to and in memory of his full and inspiring life may we each of us take time to reflect and admire this wonderful man with love, deep affection and genuine respect.'

Nicholas's ashes are buried in the garden of the splendid home in which he and Molly made so much of their final years together. Their home overlooks Lindridge's magnificent restored Italian garden – a fantastically beautiful view which gave him so much pleasure every day.

It's a great comfort to Molly that he remains so close to that view and to her and she talks to him every day. She treasures their last few weeks together, recalling:

> 'I think he knew he was going to die. He became especially attentive and wanted to sit alongside me. He was such a special man. He achieved so much but he never spoke about his achievements. He never looked back. He always wanted to move on. We had so much fun.'

Not long after Nicholas's death, Molly was suddenly and inexplicably moved to tidy up her glove drawer. It was something she never normally did. In that drawer she found a bundle of letters tied with a red ribbon. They were love letters that Nicholas had written to her many years ago when they were apart. Now she reads those letters every day.

'They are my lifeline,' she says. 'And when I die they will be cremated with me.'

~ End ~